TAKE FIVE

— and pass first time —

by Christopher Dunn

The essential independent manual for students preparing for the

Grade Five Theory of Music

examination of the Associated Board of the Royal Schools of Music

MARLBOROUGH HOUSE MUSIC

• •

Hide Hollow • Higher Ringmore Road • Shaldon • Devon • TQ14 0HH

Contents

Many thanks

My name goes on the cover, but there are several people without whose help *Take Five* wouldn't have happened.

Firstly, I'd like to thank my friend Rodney Dale who has tirelessly and generously given me help and advice on publishing. As a musician, his help has also been invaluable in reading and checking my text — and we've enjoyed some jolly good lunches in the process.

My thanks also to Pat Brandon and Joan Mallyon, both music teachers of long experience, who also kindly read my draft text, suggested improvements and gave great encouragement and support.

Maureen Law is another person who helped me enormously. I'd have been at a loss without her enthusiasm for the project and advice about the marketing and distribution end of the process.

Take Five is the product of my experience in teaching students to enjoy (I hope) music theory as well as pass their Grade 5, so I'd like to thank them for helping me develop the ideas and techniques contained in this book.

I also pay tribute to my wife, June, who was patient and forbearing while I toiled over writing *Take Five*. The nearest she came to complaint was to remark on one occasion: 'This had better be good.'

I hope sincerely that it *is* good — but that is for you, the reader, to judge. In fact my final bouquet of thanks goes to all you people who have actually bought a copy of *Take Five*. It really does make all the difference!

And a word about photocopying

Take Five is protected by copyright. This means that anyone who photocopies all or any part of this book is breaking the law. They are also breaking a bond of trust with the author who, like everyone else, relies on selling his skills in order to make his living.

So for anyone who might be tempted to slip *Take Five* into a photocopier, I have a message: every time you make a free copy of my work — or anyone else's for that matter — you are doing an honest craftsman out of his just wages. Not the sort of thing any good neighbour would want to have on his or her conscience, I trust.

Take Five – and pass first time

So you're heading towards Grade 5 on your instrument, and that means you should be thinking seriously about passing your Grade 5 Theory. The rules of the Associated Board of the Royal Schools of Music make it quite clear — you can't go beyond Grade 5 on an instrument until you've passed Grade 5 Theory of Music.

Helping you over the Grade 5 hurdle

I have written *Take Five* expressly to help you over the Grade 5 Theory hurdle. My book is designed to take the mystery out of music — and put some of the fun back in.

You'll find that, instead of the usual dry instruction that most theory books offer, *Take Five* is chock full of little tricks, devices and tips to help you learn and remember the rules and formulae of theory up to Grade 5 standard.

Building on your knowledge

Take Five deliberately spends little time on the basics. I figure that, if you're limbering up for Grade 5, it's because you are becoming more advanced in playing music or need your Grade 5 in order to continue with practical exams. So it's a fair bet that you will already have some knowledge of such things as how notes and time signatures work through learning to play your instrument.

But even if you're an absolute beginner, you'll find here all the information that you need to sit your Grade 5 Theory with confidence — and pass first time .

While *Take Five* is designed primarily for students who want to get that all-important Theory certificate, I hope that anyone who wants to find out how music works will also find it a thoroughly useful manual on the subject.

Making music more fun

There are two things I hope you will gain from this book: a Grade 5 Theory pass (better still a distinction) and the joy of discovering how the music which you play on your instrument actually works.

Who knows, what you learn from *Take Five* might even inspire you to carry on with your theory studies — right up to Grade 8 and beyond. I'd be glad if it did.

But first let's get that Grade 5 Theory ticked off !

Chris Dunn
Cambridge 1999

DEDICATION

Take Five is dedicated to my four daughters, Olivia, Silvia, Celia and Chloe, who all passed
their Grade 5 Theory first time using the methods and techniques contained in this book

Notes about notes

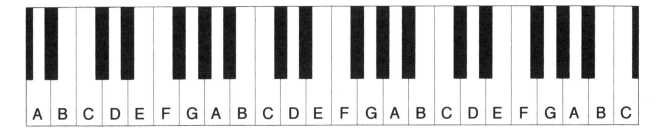

Notes — that is different musical sounds — are made by instruments or voices creating vibrations which travel through the air as sound waves. Each note vibrates at its own frequency. The higher the frequency (faster the vibration) the higher the note. And the slower the lower.

This difference is called 'pitch', *ie* the speed at which a note vibrates determines its pitch.

In music we label the pitch of notes by the first seven letters of the alphabet: A, B, C, D, E, F and G. After G we start at A again; this second A is said to be an 'octave' above the first A (*ie* the eighth letter), and all the notes which follow will be an octave above their corresponding letter names. We can then carry on to the next octave and so on upwards, depending on the range of the instrument.

Alphabetical progressions, both upwards and downwards, are called 'scales'.

You'll see from the keyboard diagram that the layout of black and white notes follows the seven-note sequence also. Wherever a G occurs, for instance, it always appears in the same relation to the pattern of black and white keys.

Before we play a musical note, there are two basic things we need to know about it:

- its pitch (what note to play)
- its duration (how long to play it for)

The pitch of a note is indicated by its position on the 'stave' (see opposite). Its duration is shown by the use of different notation symbols, each of which specifies a particular time value (note length).

Note lengths come in six basic varieties, and the note mountain below shows the way they relate. See how the value halves at each step as you go down the mountain. Students often find the more descriptive American names for the notes helpful, so I have added these in brackets.

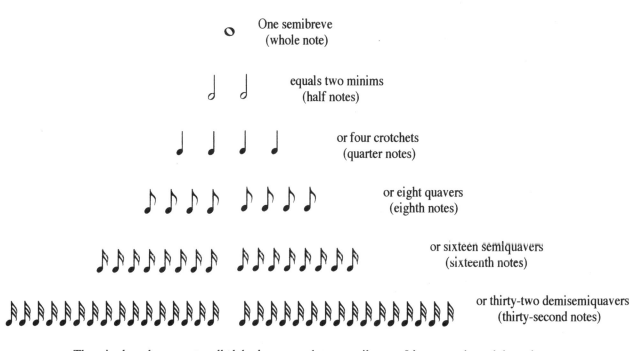

There is also a longer note called the *breve*, worth two semibreves. It's not much used these days, though it does sometimes turn up in hymns and other church music. It looks like this: ‖**O**‖

Lines and spaces

The set of five parallel lines on which notes are written is called a stave. But before we write any notes, we need to establish just what the notes on the lines and in the spaces will be. This is done with a symbol called a clef, of which there are two principal types: the G clef (usually known as the treble clef) and the F clef (usually called the bass clef). We also have to consider C clefs, but we'll leave those aside until we discuss clefs in more detail on the next page.

By placing a treble (G) clef on a stave, we fix the second line from the bottom as the note of G above middle C — that's the C right in the middle of the piano keyboard. In fact the treble clef symbol is just a fancy capital G.

Now we can write some notes:

In the bass (F) clef, the position of the F below middle C is fixed by the two dots either side of the second line from the top of the stave. As the G clef symbol is a fancy G, so the bass clef symbol is a fancy F.

Leger lines

Notes frequently go above and below the stave. For this we add short lines called leger lines. Some people spell that 'ledger' with a d, but I prefer leger because it is actually from the French word *léger*, meaning light.

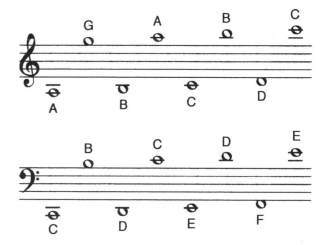

One other thing on leger lines: it can get a bit confusing for the player if the notes go way off the stave. Where music goes more than five leger lines higher than the stave, composers usually write it an octave lower and mark '*8va*' (abbreviated from the Italian *ottava*) above the passage, to show that the notes should be played an octave higher. The same goes for leger lines below the stave: written an octave higher but marked '*8va bassa*'. The instruction '*loco*' means return to the pitch as written.

Making notes

Have a go at writing some notes. Though you are familiar with reading printed and manuscript music, you may not have tried scoring it yourself. Try copying in your manuscript book a couple of rows of each type of note shown in the note mountain on the opposite page.

Be careful that you write your notes the correct way up. The rule is that the stems of notes pitched *above the middle line* of the stave should hang *downwards*. Below that

line they should point *upwards*. But *on* the middle line, for the most part you can please yourself. The same rules apply no matter what clef you may be working on.

Take a few minutes to study and practise writing the examples shown here. See how stems go on the left of the blob if hanging downwards, and to the right if upwards.

Notice also that the tails *always* go on the right hand side of the stem, regardless of whether the stem is pointing upwards or downwards.

We'll be talking on page 9 about how groups of notes which have tails can be joined together with 'beams'.

Fixing the pitch

At Grade 5 you need to know the alto and tenor clefs, as well as the treble and bass clefs which we discussed on the previous page. There are other more obscure clefs found in old music, but they needn't bother us here.

It is most important that you write your clef symbols clearly and accurately positioned on the stave. So here's your chance to practise writing clefs. The examiner will certainly penalise you for any clef that isn't clearly written in its correct position, so here's how to get it right.

Treble clef. This is the one most of us know well from playing music. As we learned on the previous page, it is also sometimes called the G clef because the curly bit fixes that line as the note of G above middle C and the symbol is based on a fancy capital G.

But how convincingly can you write a treble clef on the stave? Open your manuscript book and have a shot at it now. The best way is to start with your pencil in the middle of the F space. Make a clockwise curl around the G line, then complete the symbol with a flourish. Note that the swirls at the top and bottom extend about one leger line's worth above and below the stave.

Bass clef. If you're a pianist, you'll know it as your 'left hand' clef. Bass instrumentalists will know it too, while any musician will at least recognise the symbol from musical scores.

It is also called the F clef. The symbol is derived from an old-fashioned capital F and the two dots either side of the second line down fix that line as the F below middle C.

Draw a bass clef by starting with the little blob on the F line, then make your curl upwards to touch the line above and continue round with a sweep to complete it. Finish up with the two dots either side of the F line.

Alto clef. Viola players will know this one, but it doesn't appear often anywhere else. You are certain to meet it in a Grade 5 exam, however. The alto clef is one of the C clefs, so-called because the squiggle in the middle of the symbol fixes the line it straddles as middle C.

To draw an alto clef, start with the two vertical lines on the left. It isn't really necessary to make the first one fatter than the second but, if you're a stickler for accuracy, go ahead and thicken it up.

Look closely at the sample clef, then copy it. The most important thing is that the centre of your symbol is firmly astride the middle line to fix it as middle C. Look at the tenor clef which comes next, and you will see why it's so important to make alto and tenor clefs clearly different.

Tenor clef. Music for cellos, bassoons and trombones is sometimes written in this clef. It's another C clef, using the same symbol as the alto clef. The difference is that the tenor C clef hops *up* one line, fixing middle C as the *second* line from the top of the stave. The diagrams below will help you understand the difference.

Now that you're an expert in drawing C clef symbols from your work on the alto clef, try practising it in the tenor clef. Note that the vertical lines stand on the second line from the bottom of the stave, and extend one leger line's worth above it. Again, it is vital that the squiggle in the middle marks the correct line clearly.

Why is middle C called middle C?

Because it's plumb in the middle of the piano keyboard. It is also right 'in the middle' between the treble and the bass clefs.

In musical scores the two clefs are printed further apart than I've shown here. In reality there is just one line (middle C) between the bottom line of the treble clef (E) and the top line of the bass clef (A). Think of the two clefs as one eleven-line stave, and the relationship between treble and bass will always be quite clear in your mind.

Now look at the diagram below, showing how the alto and tenor clefs fit into the picture. You see how logically the clefs relate? Just keep in mind where middle C is on each clef. Armed with this knowledge, you'll be able to cope with even the trickiest question about note positions — especially when it comes to *transposition* (page 32).

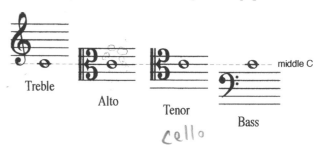

Signs for silence

We now know how to recognise the pitch of a note in any of the four clefs. And we know for how long we should play it. But what about when we're told *not* to play?

Signs which dictate breaks in the music are called rests, and are as important as notes. Just as there are six types of note value, so there are six corresponding types of rest. Have a look at how they appear on the stave, then try writing a line or two of each in your manuscript book.

I have shown them on a stave without specifying a particular clef, because the position of each type of rest on the stave is the same in every clef.

Semibreve		**Minim**	
Note	Rest	Note	Rest
Crotchet		**Quaver**	
Note	Rest	Note	Rest
Semiquaver		**Demisemiquaver**	
Note	Rest	Note	Rest

Time values for rests follow the same arithmetic as the note values with which they correspond (see the note mountain on page 4). A minim rest is equal to half a semibreve, a crotchet rest half a minim, and so on.

Spot the difference

Most rest symbols are quite clear; but be careful with semibreve and minim rests. The only difference between them is their position on the stave. The semibreve rest *hangs* below the second line from the top of the stave, while the minim sits *on* the middle line. One way of fixing the difference in your mind is to remember this: **M** for Minim. **M** for Mouse. And **M**ouse *sits on* the **M**at.

Crotchet rests are sometimes represented by a sign that looks like the quaver symbol back-to-front: ʅ. I think this can be confusing so I recommend that, when you're notating music, you always use the ξ crotchet symbol.

The breve rest

There is also a breve rest, shown on the right. It's worth two semibreves, but like the breve note (see page 4) it's not commonly used nowadays.

The breve rest does retain one small duty. In a bar marked $\frac{4}{2}$ time (we'll be talking 'time signatures' on page 9) the breve rest is used to mark a full bar's rest. In every other time signature the *semibreve* rest is used to show a whole bar rest — just one of those irritating little quirks.

Longer rests

Orchestral players often have extended rests in their parts. I once watched a french horn player dismantle his instrument, clean it and reassemble it all in the space of a 96-bar rest during a performance of Handel's *Messiah*!

Rests of longer than a couple of bars go like this:

Fairly obviously, the numbers above the stave refer to how many bars' rest should be taken. But I don't recommend that you try the horn player's cleaning and polishing routine during your orchestral performances!

Extending notes and rests

Dotted notes

A dot placed after a note tells us to extend that note by half its value again. A dotted minim, for example, is worth three crotchets. A dotted quaver means it is to be lengthened by one semiquaver (three semiquavers in all). A dotted crotchet is worth three quavers, *etc*. It's straight arithmetic really. On the stave it goes like this:

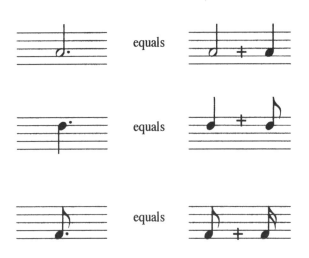

And so on; I think you get the picture. Notice how the dot is written directly *beside* a note that is in a space, but in the space *above* if the note is on a line.

Double-dotted notes

Things get slightly more complicated with double dots. A double-dotted note indicates that it should be played *three-quarters* as long again. In other words, the first dot adds half the written note's value and the second dot adds a quarter of the written note's value.

Looking at it on the stave:

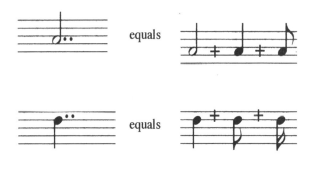

Dotted and double-dotted rests

Rests can be dotted and double-dotted as well. The same time values apply as for their corresponding notes, *eg*:

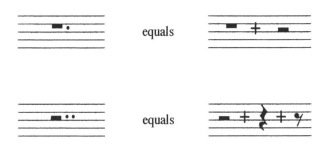

As we shall see when we get on to bar lines and time signatures, bars of music must always have their correct numbers of beats. This is when the time values of notes and rests become a critical issue.

Tying notes together

A note can also be made longer by the use of the 'tie'. For instance, instead of writing a dotted minim, you could write a minim followed by a crotchet of the same note and tie them together:

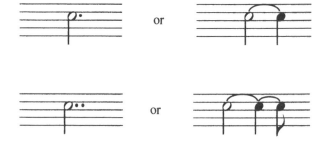

Any types of notes can be tied together (so long as they are of the same pitch of course). Don't confuse a tie with a 'slur'. The slur is a symbol used to mark passages of music or groups of notes which are to be played *legato* — the musical term for 'smoothly'. The tie simply extends the sound to whatever the total value of all the notes that are tied together.

Ties are most commonly used when a note is held across from the end of one bar and into the next (because a dotted note cannot be held over a bar line). However, we need to understand the basics about bar lines and time signatures before we can consider how the tie gets involved. If you want a preview, see page 13.

In time to the music

Bar lines are vertical lines drawn across the stave at regular intervals to divide up the music into 'bars' of equal duration. Each bar must contain exactly the right number of beats.

How many beats there should be in each bar, and what type of beats they are, is always given in an instruction at the beginning of the music. This instruction is called the *time signature*. It always appears as two numbers, one above the other, typically like this:

 The upper number tells us *how many* beats there are to be in each bar. The lower figure indicates *what type* of beats they are.

In the example here, we are told there are to be three beats to each bar — but the '**4**' underneath?

Refer back to the notes mountain on page 4 and the following will make perfect sense:

The figure **1** means **semibreve** beats
The figure **2** means **minim** beats
The figure **4** means **crotchet** beats
The figure **8** means **quaver** beats
The figure **16** means **semiquaver** beats

In practice, the **1** for semibreve beats is extremely rare these days; the ones you will meet are **2**, **4**, **8** and **16**.

So if we have a piece of music marked $\frac{2}{4}$ we know that each bar must be made up of *two crotchet* beats:

Similarly a time signature of $\frac{3}{8}$ would tell us to play three quaver beats to the bar:

As the examples show, the beats can be made up of different types of note — so long as the content of each bar adds up to the right number. Obviously rests must also be accounted for, as demonstrated in the second bar of the three/eight example.

Beaming notes together

Notes which have tails attached to their stems (*ie* any note with 'quaver' in its name) can be joined together with 'beams'. For instance, this looks a bit of a dog's dinner:

But it can be written much more clearly with beams:

While the un-beamed example would be difficult for the player to read, the beamed version shows the beats in the bar quite clearly. Notes can be beamed whether their stems go upwards or downwards, as shown by the following sample bar in three/four time:

You can also beam together notes of different types, *eg*:

Practise drawing single, double and triple beams grouping various types of notes. One other thing: *never beam notes across a bar line* — a criminal offence in music theory!

Two types of time

Time by numbers

Time signatures are described as *duple, triple, quadruple, quintuple and septuple,* depending on whether they have two, three, four, five or seven beats to the bar. It shouldn't be hard to remember:

- *Duple* means *two* beats to the bar
- *Triple* means *three* beats to the bar
- *Quadruple* means *four* beats to the bar
- *Quintuple* means *five* beats to the bar
- *Septuple* means *seven* beats to the bar

Quintuple and septuple are perhaps less common, but we still have to know how to handle them at Grade 5.

Simple time

When *each beat* within the bar is divisible by two, the music is said to be in *simple time*. For example:

Simple duple time

Simple triple time

Simple quadruple time

In each case the notes can be divided into twos — a crotchet will split into two quavers, a quaver into two semiquavers and so on.

Enter the triplet

I'm sure you will have come across triplets in your playing. That's when the composer tells you to play three notes in the time normally taken by two notes. Triplets are shown by a small *3* written above or below the relevant notes, usually with a bracket to make it absolutely clear.

The triplet is telling us to play the three (equal) quavers in the same time as two, but it doesn't alter the fact that the piece is in simple time. However, what if every note in the piece was written to be played as a triplet? It would be a bit of a mess with all those *3*s scattered everywhere. That is where *compound time* comes in.

Compound time

While in simple time each beat within the bar is divisible by two, in *compound time* each beat is divisible by *three*. There are two characteristics in compound time which make it easy to spot: 1) an abundance of dotted notes and 2) notes grouped into three. Consider the following:

If we analyse this in terms of what we said about time signatures on the previous page, we might say that the upper number (6) tells us there are six beats to the bar and the lower number (8) means they are quaver beats.

Indeed, there are six quavers to the bar. But, as the note groupings in the example above suggests, six/eight time is actually counted as *two compound beats* to the bar. Thus a six/eight time signature is compound duple.

The dictionary defines *compound* as 'mixed, or composed of a number of parts'. And, of course, that is what we have here — beats composed of a 'number of parts'.

Each simple time signature has an equivalent compound time signature. Compare these:

Both have two beats to the bar. But the two/four time has straight crotchets and the six/eight has dotted crotchets. It therefore follows with arithmetical logic that three/four time (three crotchet beats to the bar) will have an equivalent compound time of nine/eight (three *dotted* crotchets to the bar). And four/four time (four crotchet beats) will have an compound equivalent of twelve/eight (four *dotted* crotchets).

The table opposite shows time signatures you are likely to meet at Grade 5, and how they relate to one another.

TIME	SIMPLE	COMPOUND
DUPLE	(2/2, 2/4)	(6/4, 6/8, 6/16)
TRIPLE	(3/2, 3/4, 3/8)	(9/8, 9/16)
QUADRUPLE	(4/2, 4/4, 4/8)	(12/8, 12/16)
QUINTUPLE	(5/4, 5/8)	
SEPTUPLE	(7/4, 7/8)	

Odd ones out

We have already talked briefly about triplets (page 10). Knowing what you now do about the difference between simple and compound time, and about the need for the right number of notes in a bar, you might say that a triplet is a sort of simple/compound time mix. Quite right.

More technically, a triplet is known as an 'irregular time division'. And at Grade 5 a number of possible irregular time divisions can turn up.

In the first example below, we see how a triplet of crotchets is to be played in the time of one minim. And then how five semiquavers (a quintuplet) must be played in the space of four semiquavers (one crotchet):

The principal applies with irregular groups of all kinds. For instance, a 'duplet' may appear in compound time:

This tells the player to play two quavers in the same time as three (or a dotted crotchet). The number above an irregular group is often shown with a curved 'slur' to indicate the notes affected. However, I recommend the use of a square bracket; it's less confusing than the slur, which is already used in music to indicate other things.

We've looked at duplets (2), triplets (3) and quintuplets (5). Now consider sextuplets (6), septuplets (7):

The indication is that both the sextuplet and the septuplet should be played over one crotchet beat. You might also come across groups of nine (for some reason they don't have a special name). Here the nine demisemiquavers are to be played in the space of eight (one crotchet):

Grouping notes into beats

On page 9 we saw how joining notes with beams makes a melody clearer to read. In simple time you can beam notes together up to a complete bar in two/four and three/four time signatures. In four/four you can beam up to half a bar. In the following, for example, it would be wrong to carry the beam right through the bar:

In compound time notes should be beamed to show the individual beats of the bar. In the following example of compound duple time, for instance, it would be wrong to beam all six quavers together in the second bar:

Similarly, in triple and quadruple compound times, the groupings should always follow the beats of the bar.

Beaming in irregular time signatures

We have to pay special attention to the groupings of notes in the irregular time signatures. In quintuple time, the convention is to group notes either as 2 + 3, or 3 + 2:

Grouping in septuple time is more flexible: 4 + 3, or 2 + 2 + 3, or 2 + 3 + 2, or 3 + 2 + 2 are acceptable. *Eg*:

Marking time

Metronome markings and tempo

Time signatures tell us how many beats to the bar and what type of beats. What they don't say is how fast or slowly we are to play.

At the top of a piece of music you will usually see a metronome marking which indicates the speed or 'tempo' at which the composer wants it to be played. You probably know the helpful tick-tock of the metronome from your instrumental studies, but you may not know that it was invented by a man called Maelzel nearly 200 years ago. I only mention that because a metronome marking often looks like this: M.M. ♩ = 80. And 'M.M.' stands for Maelzel's Metronome.

Just as often, a metronome marking will appear simply as ♩ = 80. The message is the same. It means the piece should be played at the speed of 80 crotchets per minute.

If you consider that 60 crotchets per minute would be one crotchet per second, it's quite easy to get an idea of the tempo at which a piece of music is intended to be played. Obviously 120 crotchets a minute would be two per second, and so on.

Just as common is a metronome marking in minims or in quavers. Thus ♩ = 40 indicates a speed of 40 minims per minute and ♪ = 70 means 70 quavers to the minute.

Time signatures that time forgot

There are two time signatures which are often represented by special symbols instead of one number above another.

These symbols are survivals from earlier times but, in my view, the sooner they become extinct the better. They provide no advantage and merely add complication to a subject that's plenty complicated enough already.

My advice is not to use them if you have the choice, whether in your theory studies or when writing musical scores of your own. On the other hand, we *do* have to be able to recognise them, so should you encounter the following time signature symbols, remember that:

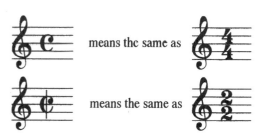

The C symbol

The **C** symbol is actually not a C at all (it's really a half circle, but we won't go into why). Nevertheless, it may help you remember that C stands for Common time, which is another name for a $\frac{4}{4}$ time signature.

You may also come across the term *alla breve*, which is another name for the time signature.

Changing times

The time signature is given only once — at the beginning of a piece of music. It remains in force until otherwise directed.

In some musical compositions the time signature changes during the piece. Any change is shown by inserting the relevant new time signature where the change of time occurs. It then remains active until it is cancelled by the appearance of another time signature.

Tying notes across a bar line

You'll recall that on page 8 we talked about tying notes together to extend them. This technique is most commonly used when we want to extend a note across a bar line. In the following example...

... the E crotchet is held for the length of a minim, but we can't write a minim, because a minim would make the bar longer than the three crotchet beats directed by the time signature.

Wherever a bar line intervenes in the middle of a note we use the tie to carry the note over into the next bar. Note the difference between the tied E across the bar line and the slur under the run of quavers that follows in the second bar. The slur is a performance direction indicating that the quavers should be played smoothly (*legato*); the tie tells us that the note is held for two crotchet beats.

One more example should be enough to make the point that notes of different value can be tied together and that tied notes can crop up in any time signature:

In black and white

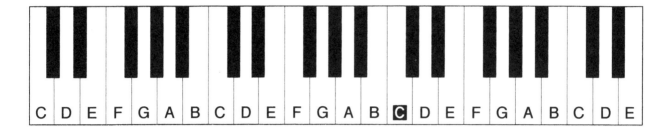

So far we have considered only 'white' notes on the keyboard. Before we get on to musical scales, we need to understand some basic things about the 'black' notes — the sharps and flats, as they are called.

Sharps

Have a look at the keyboard diagram above. The white notes are all labelled by their letter names, but where does that leave the black ones? Look at the C note I've marked. The black note to the right of it is the half-way point between the C and the D. We call it C 'sharp', which is usually abbreviated as C♯. As we shall see, that note could also be called by other names. But for the time being, C♯ it is.

Similarly, the black note that follows the D can be called D♯, then on up the scale to F♯, G♯ and A♯, bringing us to the next C♯.

Flats

For reasons which will become clearer as we get into the construction of musical scales, the black notes can also be referred to as 'flats'. The C♯ could also be called D flat or, in musical shorthand, D♭. Similarly, what we were calling D♯ a moment ago can also be regarded as E♭ and so on.

Naturals

The white notes are called 'naturals'. They are normally referred to simply by their letter names alone, with the 'natural' tag implied. But wherever there might be any doubt, we always refer to a note as being C natural, D natural and so on. The musical shorthand symbol for natural is ♮; thus: C♮, D♮, *etc.*

Notice that on the stave the sharp, flat or natural symbol comes *before* the note; but when we write about them in text the *note* comes first, ie C♯, G♭, E♮ and so on. Never place a sharp, flat or natural symbol *after* the note on a stave — it must always be written before the note.

Tones and semitones

Some more musical terminology for you. The distance between any note and its immediate neighbour, above or below, is called a 'semitone' (literally a half-tone).

From C♯ to D is a semitone (and vice versa, of course); from C♯ to C♮ is a semitone. From F to G♭ is a semitone — and so is the distance from E to F. The semitone is the basic unit of measurement in western music.

You will not be surprised to learn that two semitones makes one 'tone'. Thus the distance between G and A, for example, is a tone; A♭ to B♭ is a tone, E to F♯ is a tone and so it goes on.

The missing black notes

Notice that there is no black note between E and F, or between B and C. So is there such a thing as E♯ or B♯, F♭ or C♭? Yes there is. We frequently have to sharpen Es and Bs and flatten Fs and Cs to make music theory work.

In order to play an E♯, you would actually sound the note of F; for B♯ you'd play C. For F♭ play an E♮ and for a C♭ read B♮. Don't worry, you'll understand why once we get our heads round scales.

Enharmonic equivalents

That brings us to a general point about naming notes. Notes which make the same sound, but which must take a different name for technical reasons, are said to be *enharmonic equivalents* of one another.

B♯ is an enharmonic equivalent of C♮. E♭ and D♯ are enharmonic equivalents — and so on.

When we meet double sharps and double flats later on, you'll see how one 'note' on the keyboard can take on quite a variety of different names. But for the time being it's enough to know what we've learned here about sharps and flats to get on with the business of constructing musical scales.

A scale model for major keys

Every note, black or white, can be the starting point for a major scale. And every major scale uses a different number of sharps or flats. The major scales involved in Grade 5 are those with up to and including six sharps and six flats.

Bundles of sharps or flats may look a bit daunting, but once you understand the basic formula for constructing a major scale, they really aren't very frightening at all. With a model to work with, you can build a major scale beginning on any note of the keyboard, black or white.

A note by any other name

Each note (often called a 'degree') of a musical scale has a name, no matter what note the scale is based upon.

The **first** note of an ascending scale is called the **tonic**

The **second** is called the **supertonic**

The **third** is called the **mediant**

The **fourth** is called the **subdominant**

The **fifth** is called the **dominant**

The **sixth** is called the **submediant**

The **seventh** is called the **leading note**

And the **eighth** brings us back to the **tonic**, one 'octave' above the first tonic

The scale of C major

If someone asked you to write out the ascending scale of, say, F♯ major, where would you start? On the note of F♯, you would probably guess. But what then?

The secret, as in so many musical questions, lies in working to a model that you *do* understand. The simplest of all major scales is C major, because it has no sharps or flats, making it the easiest model to use. Pretty well everyone knows that if you start on middle C and play all the white notes up the keyboard until you hit the next C, you have the scale of C major:

C D E F G A B C

Or if you play a descending scale of C major, you play all the white notes downwards to the next C below. Any *descending* major scale uses the same notes as the ascending scale in reverse order:

C B A G F E D C

Not a sharp or a flat in sight. Now look at the notes in more detail (and especially at the notes you *don't* play).

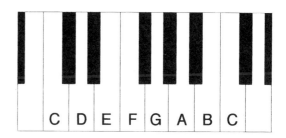

To assemble the major scale model, we analyse how many tones or semitones there are between each degree of the scale. (Remember the definitions of tones and semitones that we considered on the previous page). Check out the following against the keyboard diagram:

C to D — tone

D to E — tone

E to F — semitone

F to G — tone

G to A — tone

A to B — tone

B to C — semitone

So now we can say with absolute certainty that any ascending major scale will be built on the same model:

Tone Tone Semitone Tone Tone Tone Semitone

(or simply T T S T T T S)

And in reverse it gives us the descending scale.

This is the way C major ascending looks on the treble clef:

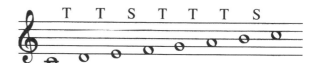

You shouldn't find it difficult to remember the formula as T T S T T T S, but if you were to forget how it goes in the heat of the exam, you know you can always work it out by building a quick scale model based on C major.

Here's a good tip: if you're asked to write a *descending* scale only, don't try to remember the formula backwards. Just begin your answer on the *last* (lowest) note of the scale and work from the last note backwards to the first.

The rungs of the ladder

A general point about scales: in major or minor scales,

each degree of the scale *must take consecutive alphabeti-cal* letter names (though they may be flattened or sharpened). Think of a scale as a ladder and the notes as rungs.

Each rung must be present, though it may be painted a different colour. In a scale, you could not have consecutive notes named as D and D♯, for example. The next rung upwards from the D would have to be an **E** *of some description* (*ie* E♭). Similarly from B to B♭ would be impossible. It must be an A♯. And so on.

The only exception is the *chromatic* scale (see page 31).

Putting the scale model to the test

We know how many semitones there have to be between each degree of the major scale. Now let's consider the major scale built on the note of A, for example.

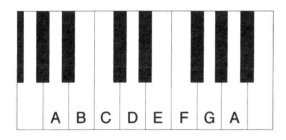

Tone	A to B
Tone	B to C♯
Semitone	C♯ to D
Tone	D to E
Tone	E to F♯
Tone	F♯ to G♯
Semitone	G♯ to A

So the scale of A major must be:

A   B   C♯   D   E   F♯   G♯   A

Of course the same T T S T T T S model will hold good for whichever major scale you build, regardless of how many sharps or flats it may involve.

Another example

Now let's put the model work on a major scale in a flat key. A♭ major, for example. Work out the tones and semitones and you should get:

Tone	A♭ to B♭
Tone	B♭ to C
Semitone	C to D♭
Tone	D♭ to E♭
Tone	E♭ to F
Tone	F to G
Semitone	G to A♭

So the scale is: A♭ B♭ C D♭ E♭ F G A♭

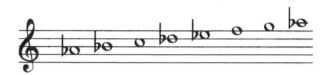

Introducing key signatures

We've discovered how sharps and flats start to appear when we construct major scales. However, a musical score would be a bit of a mess if every sharpened or flattened note had to be marked every time it occurred.

To avoid this we use a *key signature* at the beginning of each line of music, corresponding to the sharps or the flats of the scale (or 'key') in which the music is written.

Any sharp or flat which appears in the key signature affects that note at any pitch, not just at the pitch at which the key signature is actually written on the stave.

On the opposite page I have set out all the major scales we have to know at Grade 5, with their key signatures as they appear in the treble clef. (We shall see later how the relative position of key signatures on the stave changes in the alto, tenor and bass clefs.)

Time for some practice

I recommend that you have a go at putting the TTSTTTS model to work for yourself on a few major scales, without reference to what's shown on the opposite page. Once you understand how to use the model, I promise that you'll find any major scale construction a piece of cake.

C major
(no sharps
or flats)

G major
(1 sharp)

F major
(1 flat)

D major
(2 sharps)

B♭ major
(2 flats)

A major
(3 sharps)

E♭ major
(3 flats)

E major
(4 sharps)

A♭ major
(4 flats)

B major
(5 sharps)

D♭ major
(5 flats)

F♯ major
(6 sharps)

G♭ major
(6 flats)

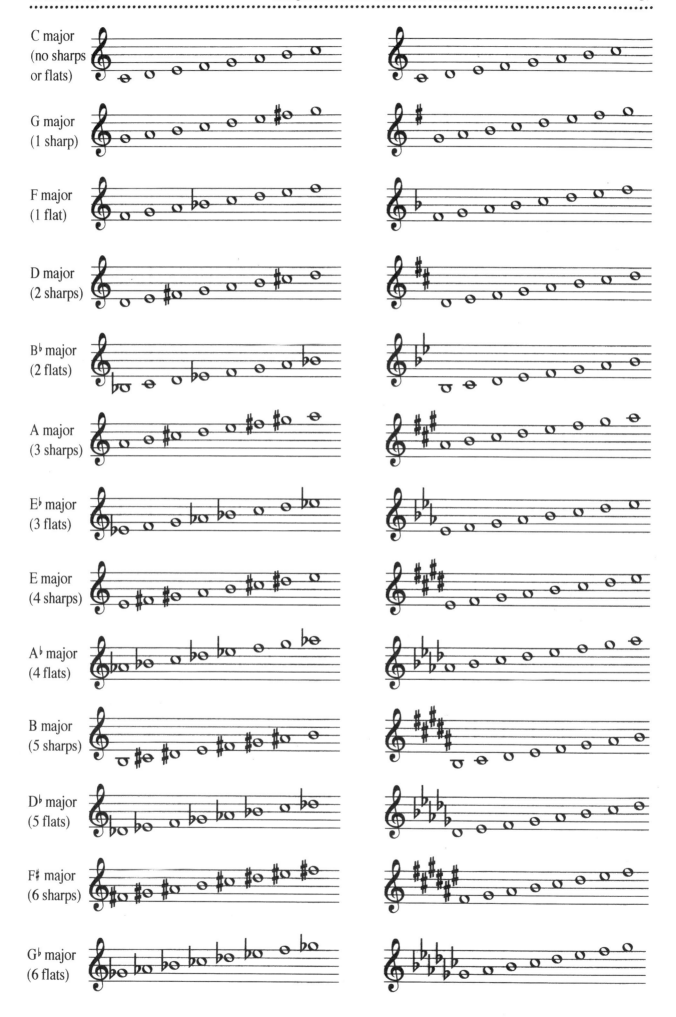

Secrets of the magic circle

Now that we understand how major scales are built, we need next to see how the different keys relate to one another. We know that C major has no sharps or flats and that in other keys we end up with whole bundles of either sharps or flats — but what's the logic behind this?

For the answer to that we turn to the Circle of Fifths, a wonderful device which demonstrates better than anything the elegant mathematical precision of music.

But before we explore the secrets of the magic Circle of Fifths, we have to define…

What we mean by 'fifths'

We are going to consider *intervals* (the way we measure the distance between different notes) in a later chapter (page 24). But, as something of a preview, we have to learn a bit here about an interval called a *fifth* before we launch into our main subject.

Take the note of C and call it number one. Now count the letter names which come after C. Number two will be D, three is E, four is F, five is G and so on. In music theory we say the interval between C and G is a 'fifth'.

Now count the number of semitones contained between the notes of C and G. You should get seven.

We have established that a fifth spans five letter names and seven semitones. So what would be the fifth above G? By counting in the same way we can see that it is D (five letter names, seven semitones). Carrying on, a fifth above D lands you on A — and so on through E and B to F♯.

Talking tetrachords

A tetrachord is the name given to a group of four consecutive notes (*tetra* means *four* in Greek). To see tetrachords in action, take the scale of C major as the model:

```
C D E F   G A B C
1 2 3 4   5 6 7 8
```

CDEF is the first tetrachord; GABC is the second. They are both built identically (tone-tone-semitone). Now look back to page 17 and notice that the first sharp key (ie with one sharp in its key signature) is G major. G is the first note of the second tetrachord of C major, a fifth above the tonic (C).

Now let's use the model to examine the tetrachords in the scale of G major:

```
G A B C   D E F♯ G
1 2 3 4   5 6 7  8
```

From this we can confidently predict that the next sharp key (two sharps) is going to be D major — the first note of the second tetrachord and a fifth above G. Back on page 17 again we see that, sure enough, two sharps (F♯ and C♯) signifies the key of D major.

Now you do it. Set out the notes of D major as I have — what's the first note of the second tetrachord? A. So the next in sequence must be A major with three sharps (F♯, C♯ and G♯). Carry on in the same way and you will find the sequence of major keys continues through E, B and F♯.

Next try this: if we know that the note of C is going to be the *first* note in the *second* tetrachord of some other major scale, what will that scale be? If the second tetrachord is CDEF then the first begins on which note? Must be F. Back once more to page 17 and we notice at once that F major is the first of the flat keys:

```
F G A B♭   C D E F
1 2 3 4    5 6 7 8
```

By using the same reverse process from F, you'll find that the flat keys roll out one by one: B♭, E♭, A♭, D♭, G♭.

There's an important point to be made here: some students get confused initially by this system of tetrachords. They assume that, for example, the scale of F major can only begin on the F below middle C; and that the scale of B♭ can only begin a fifth lower than that, and so on. But imagine playing a piece in four sharps or flats if it were so — you'd be falling off one or other end of the keyboard! A scale can be played at any pitch.

All of which brings us, at last, to the main event…

The Circle of Fifths

At the top of the next column we have the basic Circle of Fifths, showing only the major keys at this stage. I have only shown the keys involved at Grade 5 (*ie* up to six sharps and six flats). The sharp keys go in the clockwise direction and the flats anticlockwise.

Think of the Circle of Fifths as a clockface with the note of C at 12 o'clock. Travelling clockwise in fifths, we get G at one o'clock. The fifth above G gives us D at two o'clock, A at three, E at four and so on.

Whether calculating by fifths (five letter names, seven semitones) or by tetrachords, each new key appears in order. Note that when we get to the fifth above B, a sharp appears for the first time: B to F is five letter names and

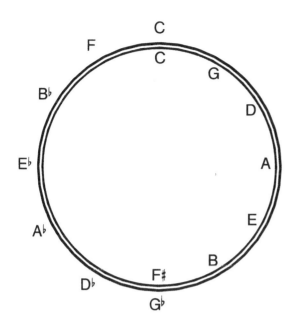

seven semitones lands us on F♯.

Now go back to C and travel anticlockwise. Using the tetrachord concept we get F at 11 o'clock B♭ at 10 o'clock and so on until we arrive at G♭ (six o'clock) — where an extremely interesting thing happens…

In the clockwise sequence we get F♯ at six o'clock, while coming the other way in the sequence of flats we have arrived at G♭ — in other words, the same note on the keyboard! As we know from page 14, the notes F♯ and G♭ are *enharmonic equivalents*.

Harmony round the clock

Now let's consider what would happen if we were to travel onwards clockwise in fifths from six o'clock. The next note in the sequence is C♯, which shares its place at seven o'clock with D♭ coming the other way. Again C♯ and D♭ are enharmonic equivalents.

If you carry on with your theory studies to Grade 6, you'll meet up with keys with seven sharps and flats, which complete the full set of scales; but at Grade 5 we don't have to concern ourselves with them.

But, for the sake of interest, carry on round the clock in fifths and see how each space would be shared by enharmonic equivalents until you get up to B♯ at 12 o'clock, which is of course an enharmonic equivalent of C.

We'll be returning to the magic circle again when we get on to minor scales. As we shall discover, it also provides a perfect picture of how the minor scales relate both to the major keys and to one another.

Here we go gathering sharps and flats

We've seen how sharps and flats start to appear when we construct major scales.

Now let's be a bit more orderly about it and work our way round the Circle of Fifths. Starting with C (no sharps or flats) and travelling clockwise we come first to G. If you use the major scale model (TTSTTTS) to construct the scale of G major, you'll find that one sharp appears — F♯.

Move on by another fifth to D. Build its major scale and a second sharp appears. In addition to the F♯ we also now have C♯. Travel on to A and we find three sharps — F♯, C♯ and G♯. Do you see how, as we progress round the circle in fifths, we keep gathering a new sharp to add to the ones we've already got? Set out as a table it looks like this:

G major:	**F♯**
D major:	F♯ **C♯**
A major:	F♯ C♯ **G♯**
E major:	F♯ C♯ G♯ **D♯**
B major:	F♯ C♯ G♯ D♯ **A♯**
F♯ major:	F♯ C♯ G♯ D♯ A♯ **E♯**
(C♯ major:	F♯ C♯ G♯ D♯ A♯ E♯ **B♯**)

You will understand when we get on to the next page why I have added in brackets the key of C♯ major, though this last sharp key doesn't appear until Grade 6. Similarly, below I have included C♭ major, the last of the flat keys.

So now let's start again at C and go anticlockwise. When we construct the major scale of F, a B♭ appears. Ever onwards, we find that in the scale of B♭ a second flat appears — E♭. And so on, like this:

F major:	**B♭**
B♭ major:	B♭ **E♭**
E♭ major:	B♭ E♭ **A♭**
A♭ major:	B♭ E♭ A♭ **D♭**
D♭ major:	B♭ E♭ A♭ D♭ **G♭**
G♭ major:	B♭ E♭ A♭ D♭ G♭ **C♭**
(C♭ major:	B♭ E♭ A♭ D♭ G♭ C♭ **F♭**)

Notice that by convention, there's never a mix of sharps and flats in a key signature. Keys are quite distinct as either *sharp* keys or *flat* keys.

Now turn over the page and meet someone who is always a good friend to theory students: Father Charles.

Into battle with Father Charles

Father Charles Goes Down And Ends Battle.
Battle Ends And Down Goes Charles's Father.

Remember these two silly sentences and you will never be at a loss with scales and key signatures. The initial letters of the first sentence (FCGDAEB) appear in reverse in the second sentence (BEADGCF). Together they give you a sequence that is one of the essential building blocks of musical construction. This sequence appears constantly whenever anything to do with scales crops up.

Have a look at the Circle of Fifths shown below. (I've included the minor keys as well. Though we won't be tackling minors until a little later, they are integrally involved in the Circle of Fifths). Notice how the sequence

of F C G D A E B (Father Charles Goes Down And Ends Battle) shows up as you move clockwise round any of the three circles. And anticlockwise the sequence is always B E A D G C F (Battle Ends And Down Goes Charles's Father). Look back also at the tables of sharps and flats on the previous page. You'll see even more clearly how our battling friend Father Charles dominates the proceedings.

Wherever you happen to be in the Circle of Fifths, armed with your silly sentences you can always predict what the letter names of neighbouring keys are going to be — also the sharps and flats in their key signatures.

A note of caution, however: Father Charles tells you the *letter* names, but he doesn't indicate any sharps or flats that may be involved. That bit's up to you.

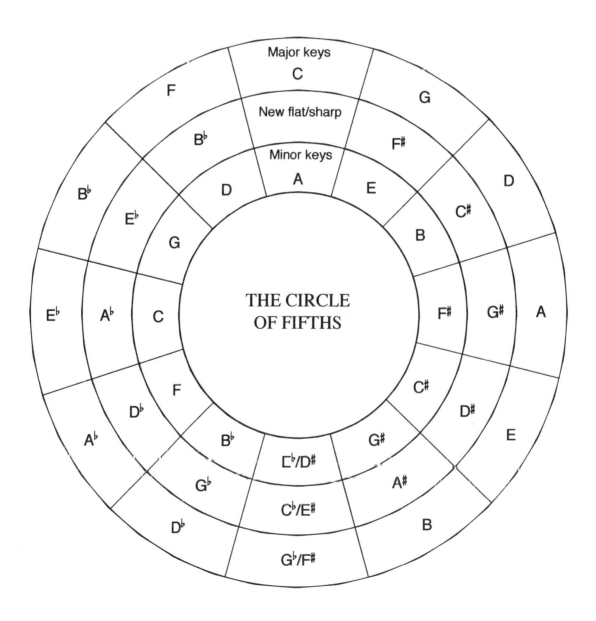

Putting key signatures in their place

On page 16 we looked at key signatures. At that stage they were shown only as they appear on the treble clef. Now, how about the alto, tenor and bass clefs?

The positioning of flats or sharps in a key signature is most important. The first point to note is that sharps and flats always assemble in the same sequence. For that sequence we have only to revisit Father Charles, who we met on the opposite page. The sharps gather as **Father Charles Goes Down And Ends Battle**. The order of the flats is **Battle Ends And Down Goes Charles's Father**.

The key signature is positioned according to the stave on which it is written. In the examples given at the foot of the page you can see that in the treble clef the key signature is placed above middle C, while in the alto and tenor clefs it is positioned around middle C and in the bass it appears below middle C. It might be helpful here to recall that diagram of clef positions that we looked at earlier.

Each flat or sharp marked in the key signature affects all notes of that particular name, not just the ones which occupy the line or space which is marked.

Key signatures often change in the course of a piece of music. When that happens the composer will use a double bar line and insert the new key signature, which cancels out the previous instruction and remains in force until a new key signature appears.

Beware the tenors!

Notice how the sharps and flats are all set in the same pattern on the treble, alto and bass clefs, always in the same sequence. The rogue is the tenor clef. While the *flats* are set in the same pattern as they are in the three other clefs, the *sharps* appear in a different arrangement — though in the same sequence. Another one of those 'exceptions to the rule' — and one of those things which can lose you marks needlessly in the exam if you get it wrong.

It is enough to show here how the key signatures stack up in six sharps and six flats in order to demonstrate the relative positions. For key signatures with fewer sharps or flats, simply deduct as necessary. I suggest you practise writing key signatures in your manuscript book. A scrappy or inaccurate key signature will unsettle an examiner!

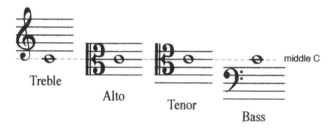

Treble   Alto   Tenor   Bass   middle C

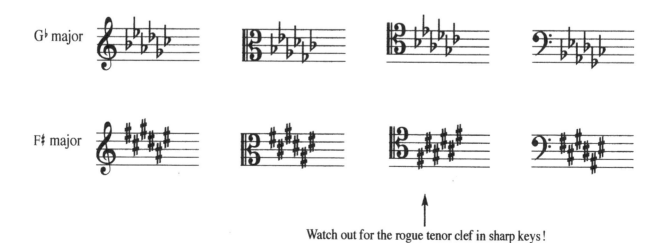

G♭ major

F♯ major

Watch out for the rogue tenor clef in sharp keys!

Accidentals in action

You will have met accidentals frequently while playing music. They are the notes which the composer sharpens or flattens to add colour and variety to the key in which a piece is written. The piece may be in D major (two sharps in the key signature), for example, but you can expect to encounter some notes which have been individually sharpened, flattened or 'naturalised'.

These are called accidentals.

You will know well the symbols for sharps, flats and naturals. Less familiar may be the double sharps and double flats, so it's worth pausing here to establish how accidentals work and the rules which govern them.

Accidentals come in five varieties:

♯	sharp	*raises a note by one semitone*
♭	flat	*lowers a note by one semitone*
x	double sharp	*raises a note by two semitones*
♭♭	double flat	*lowers a note by two semitones*
♮	natural	*restores to natural pitch a note that has been either sharpened or flattened*

The basic rules for all accidentals

If a note is altered by an accidental, the alteration remains in force until the end of the bar in which it occurs, unless otherwise stated. Consider this:

The naturalised C remains in force until the end of the first bar, covering the semiquaver as well. However, the note at the beginning of the second bar reverts to C♯ automatically, because the bar line cancels the instruction.

Sometimes a composer will ignore the bar-line rule, if he or she thinks the intention isn't quite clear. For example:

The restored C♯ is not technically necessary, but who are we to tell the composer his/her business? For us the rule holds firm, however: the bar line cancels the instruction unless otherwise specified.

That brings us to another scenario:

Here the tie across the bar line tells us that the C natural continues; there is no need to mark the new C as natural. But if there were no tie, under the bar line rule it *would* be necessary to plant a ♮ in front of the new C, if it is still to be naturalised.

If the same note appears again later in the bar, then it must be marked. In the example below, the C natural is carried over from the previous bar, but the second C natural has been correctly marked.

Another key point: *accidentals don't jump octaves.* The accidental applies only to the note *at that pitch.* In the example below, the middle C an octave lower would read as C♯ unless marked as a C♮ as it is here.

Accurate accidentals

Always draw your accidentals very carefully on the stave. It's so easy to lose exam marks because what you have written is not clear, and accidentals are particularly prone to accidents in this respect. Hand-written sharps and naturals can look quite similar, for example. It is also easy to place an accidental uncertainly. So *be accurate.*

Sharps

A sharp accidental raises the note by a semitone:

Here the C natural is raised by a semitone to become C♯, the F is sharpened to F♯, and the D to D♯.

Flats

A flat accidental lowers the note by a semitone:

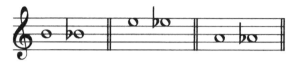

The B natural is lowered by a semitone to become B♭, the E is flattened to E♭ and the A becomes A♭. And so on.

Double sharps

The double sharp raises the note by *two* semitones. In practice it only occurs where a note which is already sharpened by the key signature needs to be sharpened by a further semitone. As we shall see when we get on to minor scales it is necessary to double sharpen Fs and Cs in some instances in order to preserve the 'rungs of the ladder' rule about using consecutive letter names.

Unlike the double flat, which repeats the flat symbol twice (see below), the double sharp has its own symbol, usually drawn in manuscript as a small x.

In the first example above, the F♯ directed by the key signature is raised a second semitone by the double sharp accidental. And of course F✗ sounds the same note as G♮ on the keyboard. In the second example, the C♯ becomes C✗ (raised by two semitones, it will sound the same note as D on the piano).

Double flats

The double flat lowers the note by two semitones. Like the double sharp, it usually applies to a note that has already been flattened by a semitone in the key signature:

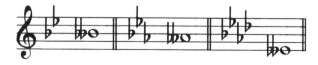

The B♭ directed by the key signature becomes B♭♭ (same note on the piano as A); A♭ in the second example becomes A♭♭, (keyboard G); and the E♭ in the third example becomes E♭♭ (keyboard D).

Naturals

A natural can be used in two ways. It can be an accidental in its own right, flattening or sharpening a note which is included in the key signature. It is also used to restore a note changed by another accidental to its former status.

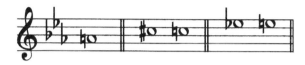

The A♭ in the key signature of the first example becomes A♮; the C♯ in the second drops a semitone to C♮, and the E♭ in the third example is sharpened to become E♮.

Naturalising double sharps/flats

Don't use a natural symbol when restoring double sharps or double flats to their former status. The convention (and that means the rule for us at Grade 5) is to use single sharps or flats. Take a look at this:

The F double sharp is simply restored to its key signature status by the use of a single sharp. Some composers still use the old method of putting in a natural as well (*ie* ♮♯ or ♮♭). But at Grade 5 we go with the modern standard and use the single sharp or flat for the job:

Sunny intervals

In music, an 'interval' is described as the difference in pitch between two notes. We have to be able to measure intervals extremely accurately. In order to understand how it's done, let's first look at the keyboard.

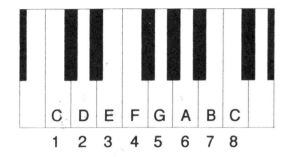

Every interval has a double-barrelled name. One part of the name is always a number; the other describes what sort of number it is. First let's tackle how the numbers part of it works.

Intervals by numbers

If you recall what we learned about fifths when talking about the Circle of Fifths, it won't come as any surprise to discover that, in the keyboard layout above, from C to D is called a *second*; D is the *second* letter counting onwards from C. And you can probably guess that from C to E is called a *third* because E is the third degree, C to F is a *fourth*, and so on.

Within an octave we have seven possible intervals:

2nd   3rd   4th   5th   6th   7th   8th
(the 8th is usually known as 8ve for 'octave')

These intervals can be used to describe the relationships between any two notes. For instance the interval between D and E is a 2nd, from F to B is a 4th, from G to E is a 6th, B to D is a 3rd, E to B a 5th, *etc.*

When counting to work out intervals, always include *both* letter names in your calculation (*eg* from G to E covers six letter names G-A-B-C-D-E, so it's a 6th).

Beyond the octave

So what about intervals of more than an octave? At Grade 5 we are expected to know intervals between any two notes, which may well take us further than an 8ve.

Intervals which go beyond the first octave can be labelled in one of two ways. An interval of a 9th, for example, can be called either 9th or *compound 2nd*. The 10th is also known as a compound 3rd, and so on up to the 15th (compound 8ve).

You can use whichever name you prefer (but stick with one, rather than mixing them). Personally I prefer to use the compound system; it's easier to think in octaves.

This is the way intervals line up based on middle C:

Intervals by type

So much for the numbers. Next we have to learn to identify the variety of interval types that are possible *within* each number. We must now think of an interval as being a 3rd, 6th, or whatever — *of some description*.

There are five types of interval that concern us:

major ✓
minor ✓
perfect
augmented
diminished

Major intervals and perfect intervals

In order to define major and perfect intervals, let's consider a C major scale. We know that what the model tells us about intervals will also be true of any other major scale, no matter how many sharps or flats in the key signature.

As you would expect in a *major* scale, the intervals it contains are *major* intervals. Except that it's not quite so simple as that! While we talk happily of major 2nds, major 3rds, major 6ths and major 7ths, by convention 4ths, 5ths and 8ves are always known as *perfect* intervals.

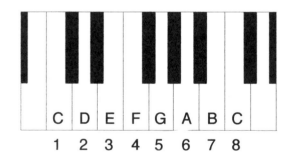

Working from the note of C, the 'white note' intervals are:

C to D	major 2nd
C to E	major 3rd
C to F	perfect 4th
C to G	perfect 5th
C to A	major 6th
C to B	major 7th
C to C	perfect 8ve

Now we're going to analyse that in terms of the semitones contained within each major and perfect interval:

C to D	major 2nd	two semitones
C to E	major 3rd	four semitones
C to F	perfect 4th	five semitones
C to G	perfect 5th	seven semitones
C to A	major 6th	nine semitones
C to B	major 7th	eleven semitones
C to C	perfect 8ve	twelve semitones

So we now have a model for all major and perfect intervals. We know that whatever the given note, we can work out any major or perfect interval above or below it.

For example, if asked for the major 3rd above E♭, the thinking goes like this: the 3rd must be a G *of some description* (three letter names). We know (or can easily work out from the C major scale model if we don't know it by heart) that a major 3rd contains four semitones, so the major 3rd above E♭ must be G natural.

Another example: what about a perfect 5th below G♯? Count down five letter names and we get to a C of some description. We know that the perfect 5th must contain seven semitones... count them out... must be C♯.

Minor, augmented and diminished intervals

Now that we know how major and perfect intervals work, we can put that knowledge into action on sorting out minor, augmented and diminished intervals.

Here's a useful diagram I developed to demonstrate the relationships between the five types of interval:

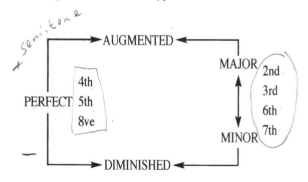

Working from the two known points on the diagram, 'perfect' and 'major', we can calculate other intervals very easily. Quite simply, each type of interval is one semitone away from its neighbour.

Deduct one semitone from a major interval and we get a minor interval. Add a semitone to a major and it becomes augmented. Reduce a perfect interval by one semitone and we have a diminished interval. A minor interval increased by one semitone becomes a major. And so it goes on. Here's the diagram again, to save you looking back to the previous page.

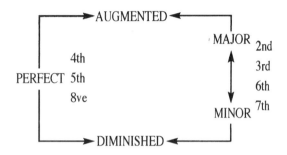

I urge you to memorise this diagram. It really does help to take the mystery out of intervals.

Let's try putting it to work on some examples.

We know (or if we don't we can pretty soon work it out by modelling) that from C to E is a major 3rd: three letter names; four semitones. From C to E♭ is still a 3rd, but it has one fewer semitones. A quick glance at the intervals model and we know that it must be a minor 3rd (three semitones). Now how about this?

The C to E♭ is a minor 3rd, as we have just worked out. From C to D♯ we can instantly recognise as a 2nd *of some description* (two letter names). A major 2nd contains two semitones, but this interval has three semitones, so it takes a step up from the major — must be an *augmented* 2nd.

I'm sure it hasn't escaped your notice that the D♯ and the E♭ sound the same on the piano. They are *enharmonic equivalents*; that is they use the same note on the keyboard (enharmonic equivalents, see page 14). But if we're

talking intervals, you can see that the difference between D♯ and E♭ is critical. Another example based on C:

C to G includes five letter names (C-D-E-F-G) and it has seven semitones. So it's a perfect 5th. C to G♭ still has five letter names, but one fewer semitones. Take one step down from 'perfect' on the intervals diagram. Clearly, C to G♭ is a diminished 5th.

If the interval were from C to F♯ (an enharmonic equivalent of G♭) then the interval would be a 4th of some description (four letter names). It includes six semitones, one more than a perfect 4th, so it's one step up from perfect to become an augmented 4th.

Let's consider an example of a compound interval:

C to A♭ has to be a 6th of some description, but this A♭ is an octave higher, so it must be a *compound* 6th of some description. C to A is a major 6th; a glance at the intervals diagram tells us that from C to A♭ must be a minor 6th. So the interval shown is a compound minor 6th. Or you could call it a minor 13th, if you prefer.

Inverted intervals

We'll be talking about inversion of intervals later (page 39). However, there's a quick point I want to make here:

An interval is said to be inverted when the root note (the one at the bottom) is moved up an octave.

In the example here we have middle C as the root and the G a perfect 5th above it. When inverted, the C hops up an octave. See how the interval now changes from a perfect 5th to a perfect 4th. More on this later.

Meet the relatives

You must be familiar with the difference in sound and feel between major and minor keys from playing scales on your instrument. While major keys sound quite cheerful and at one with the world, the minors create a sadder, more wistful impression.

The chief reason for this switch of mood between majors and minors is the difference in the third note of the scale. In a major scale, the interval between the tonic and the mediant is a major 3rd. In a minor scale the 3rd is flattened by a semitone to become a minor 3rd — altogether a less cheery-sounding interval.

There are two types of minor scale that we have to know at Grade 5 — melodic and harmonic. But before we get into all that, we need to understand a thing or two about minor keys and how they relate to the major keys.

Relative majors, relative minors

Each major key pairs up with a minor key — called its *relative minor*. And in a minor key, we refer to its *relative major*. Indeed, a relative major and minor are so closely related that they share the same key signature.

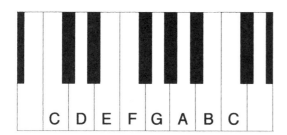

Any minor scale always begins on (and therefore takes its name from) the *minor 3rd* below the tonic of its relative major scale. In the case of C major, for example, the relative minor is called A minor (or 'Am' as it is sometimes written) because it starts on the note of A — the minor 3rd below C.

By the same token, to find a relative major scale, you would count a minor 3rd upwards from the tonic of the minor scale.

Students often make the mistake of calculating *downwards* to identify a relative major instead of upwards and the other way about for minors. This might help you avoid the problem: remember that a miner (minor) digs down and that a major gets promoted upwards.

Tell-tale sixths and sevenths

There is one other crucial factor which differentiates the notes in a minor scale from those of its relative major — and which makes minor keys easy to spot in music. In the harmonic minor scale the seventh note is sharpened by one semitone, appearing as an accidental. In the melodic minor, the sixth note is sharpened as well as the seventh in the ascending scale. Sounds complicated? Don't worry, all will be revealed when we discuss harmonic and melodic minors — coming shortly.

Father Charles in minor mode

Remember the Circle of Fifths, from page 20? Here I have shown a simplified version of it, indicating how the relative majors and minors relate round the clock-face. And of course we can at once see Father Charles battling away:

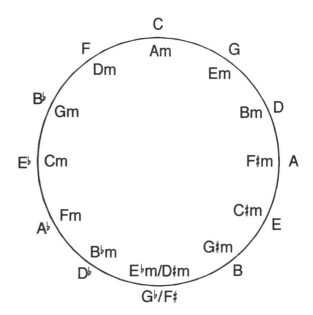

Taking A minor (Am) as your datum point (relative minor of C major at 12 o'clock) you can predict how the minor keys are going to roll out simply by referring to the Father Charles model. Take care, however, to consider any sharps or flats that may occur; no problem so long as you're careful to calculate in perfect 5ths. Of course, you will find each minor key appears in the same position on the circle as its relative major.

Note also that when you arrive at six o'clock you find D♯m and E♭m sharing that position. You've probably already spotted that they are enharmonic equivalents.

A model for harmonic minors

We analysed the scale of C major (no sharps or flats) to establish the formula T T S T T T S, which tells us how to construct a major scale. We're now going to do the same with its relative minor, A minor, to find the formula for harmonic minor scales.

First let's look at how A minor appears on the stave:

Remember there are no sharps or flats in the key signature for A minor. So the immediate question is: what's that G♯ doing there? The reason is that the seventh, or leading note, of the harmonic minor scale is always sharpened by a semitone — and it always appears as an *acci - dental*, never in the key signature. These accidentals help make minors easy to spot when you're studying a piece of music.

Now we'll analyse the tones and semitones involved so we can establish a reliable model for harmonic minors.

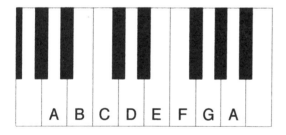

It goes like this:

A to B — tone
B to C — semitone
C to D — tone
D to E — tone
E to F — semitone
F to G♯ — one-and-a-half tones (or three semitones)
G♯ to A — semitone

That leap of three semitones (augmented 2nd) between the sixth and seventh degree is an unmistakable characteristic of the harmonic minor scale. Try playing the scale of A minor on the piano; listen to the plaintive effect created by the minor 3rd and the sharpened 7th.

So now we have the model for harmonic minors. It goes:

$$T \quad S \quad T \quad T \quad S \quad 1\frac{1}{2} \quad S$$

That may seem more difficult to remember than the model for the major scale. But, true to form in this book, we have a silly sentence to help you remember it:

Tim Sang The Theme Song in One-and-a-Half Seconds

By remembering that, or simply T S T T S 1½ S, you will be able to construct a harmonic minor in any key on demand. If you forget it, you can always come back to the A minor model with its accidental G♯ and work it out.

From top to bottom

Like the major scale, the harmonic minor scale uses the same notes descending as it does ascending. As we shall see on page 30, that is not the case with *melodic* minor scales. Here's the scale of A minor harmonic descending:

Tip number one : When writing a descending scale, don't try to remember the formula in reverse. Just begin your answer on the *last* (lowest) note of the scale and work backwards to the top.

Tip number two : Keep in mind that every major and minor scale comprises eight notes and always ends on the tonic. If you were working out a scale based on F♯, for example, its last note must be F♯ an octave above (or below). Use this knowledge to check any scale you write. If it doesn't arrive at the octave after eight notes, you can tell there's something wrong.

Tip number three : Remember the 'rungs of the ladder' idea from page 15/16? When you're writing out a scale, first put in all the letter name notes (leaving enough space between them to add any sharps, flats, naturals, double sharps or double flats that may arise).

For example, if you are starting on the note of G in an ascending scale, decide where on the stave to position the scale (go for the minimum number of leger lines); write your G, then an A, B, C and so on up to the octave G. The point is, you know that each degree of the scale will take consecutive alphabetical names. They may well be sharpened or flattened, but you know from the start that G must be followed by an A *of some description*, A by a B *of some description*, and so on, up or down the scale.

Putting Tim to the test

Now let's put Tim to work on another harmonic minor scale, just to check that you can work the system properly. Pick any minor key at random — okay, G minor.

First we need to know where we are with the key signature. What is the relative major of G minor? Count upwards three letter names: G-A-B; must be a B of some description. Count three semitones: it has to be B♭.

You could just as easily arrive at the correct key signature for G minor by starting on the note of G and applying the T S T T S 1½ S formula. So let's do it by that method:

Tone	G to A
Semitone	A to B♭
Tone	B♭ to C
Tone	C to D
Semitone	D to E♭
1½ tones	E♭ to F♯
Semitone	F♯ to G

The scale of G minor is thus:

G   A   B♭   C   D   E♭   F♯   G

On the stave it goes like this:

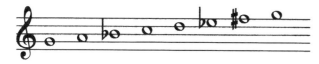

And with key signature:

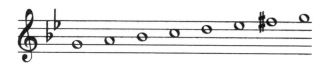

Handling naturals

Notice that once you get into minor keys of three flats and beyond, the leading note's accidental becomes a *natural*,

rather than a sharp. It's important to bear this in mind when you're writing out a scale without a key signature.

An example: in the scale of C harmonic minor, the key signature gives three flats (B♭, E♭ and A♭). If we call in Tim, we can work out that the scale will go:

C   D   E♭   F   G   A♭   B(♮)   C

Though we have B♭ in the key signature, we have sharpened it to a B natural to create the augmented 2nd between A♭ and B. If you write the scale *without* a key signature, there is no need to add the natural accidental. It simply goes:

But with key signature, the accidental becomes essential:

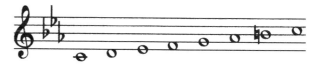

Enter the double sharp

In keys containing five sharps (G♯ minor) and beyond, the leading note takes a *double sharp*. For example, using the Tim routine, the key of G♯ harmonic minor goes:

G♯   A♯   B   C♯   D♯   E   F✕   G♯

We already have F♯ in the key signature, but in order to make the augmented 2nd between the sixth note (E) and the seventh, we have to *double* sharpen it. The F✕ is enharmonically equivalent to G natural, giving us the final semitone step to the tonic, G♯. That way, the 'rungs of the ladder' that we've talked about are preserved.

Without key signature, it looks like this on the stave:

And with key signature:

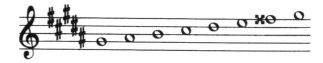

Modelling the melodic minor

Why have two types of minor scale? The simple answer is that the harmonic form suits the needs of harmony (the way chords work) while the melodic minor is more in tune with the requirements of melody writing.

And you thought we had two types of minor just to make life more difficult! Don't worry. If you coped with harmonic minors, you'll find the melodic form drops into place with no problem once you understand the differences between the harmonic and melodic forms.

Again we shall use A minor as our model for the melodic, because it has no sharps or flats in the key signature. First let's compare the two different forms of A minor alphabetically, ascending and descending:

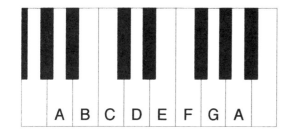

Harmonic

A B C D E | F G♯ | A | G♯ F | E D C B A

Melodic

A B C D E | F♯ G♯ | A | G♮ F♮ | E D C B A

It's immediately clear from this, and the notated comparison shown below, that all the action centres on the sixth

and seventh degrees of the scale. In the melodic form the sixth and seventh notes are sharpened in the rising scale, but not in the descending scale. The comparison, both alphabetically and on the stave, demonstrates how harmonic and melodic minors differ in two ways:

1 The harmonic minor has its seventh note sharpened by an accidental in both the ascending and descending scales. The melodic minor uses accidentals *only* in the ascending scale; it has *no accidentals* in the descending scale.

2 The harmonic minor has the sharpened seventh. In the melodic minor the *sixth* degree of the ascending scale is sharpened as well as the seventh (but neither sixth nor seventh are sharpened in the descending scale). The effect is to   remove the characteristic augmented second of the harmonic minor and make a smoother progression in melody.

That is how harmonic and melodic minors *differ*. It is also useful to bear in mind how they are alike:

• The first five notes of the ascending scale (the last five of the descending) are the same in both the harmonic and melodic forms. That includes the minor 3rd we met in the harmonic form, of course, which provides the characteristic 'minor' sound.

• Like the harmonic, the melodic minor takes the key signature of the relative major. The sharpened and flattened 6ths and 7ths appear only as accidentals.

(The accidentals in the descending melodic minor scale are technically unnecessary, because the bar line automatically cancels the accidentals in the previous bar. I have inserted naturals to make it absolutely clear how the descending scale behaves)

So let's get model-making

Take a look at the melodic scale of A minor at the foot of the previous page. Let's see how it breaks down:

A to B   — tone
B to C   — semitone
C to D   — tone
D to E   — tone
E to F♯   — tone
F♯ to G♯   — tone
G♯ to A   — semitone

Notice that the first five degrees of the scale are the same as for the harmonic. The only change is that the sixth note (F) is sharpened to smooth out the augmented second (three semitones) that occurs in the harmonic.

That's the model for the ascending melodic minor, but of course it behaves differently in descending mode:

A to G   — tone
G to F   — tone
F to E   — semitone

E to D   — tone
D to C   — tone
C to B   — semitone
B to A   — tone

See how the descending scale uses only white notes on the piano keyboard. From this you can deduce that any melodic minor scale descending will use only the sharps or flats which appear in the key signature.

Remembering the formula

I leave it to you whether or not to remember the formula by inventing your own silly sentence like we did with Tim in the harmonic scale.

I generally find it easier to remember the Tim formula for the harmonic form, knowing that I have to sharpen the sixth as well in the ascending melodic. Also that the descending melodic scale has no accidentals (only the sharps or flats contained in the key signature).

I recommend that you go back to page 23 and read again about handling naturals and double sharps, which is equally relevant to melodic and harmonic forms.

A dash of colour with chromatic scales

You probably know the chromatic scale from your instrumental studies. It's the one that rises or falls from a given note to its octave in semitones (using every black key and white key on the keyboard).

The major and minor scales we have looked at so far are all known as 'diatonic' scales. It comes from a Greek word meaning 'through the tones'.

'Chromatic' means coloured. It actually sounds pretty dull and unmusical when played as a scale, but can create interesting effects when used sparingly in musical composition, especially in a concerto for instance, giving the soloist a chance to show off his or her lightning technique.

There are two basic points to watch when notating chromatic passages:

1. Watch out for the key signature, if one is given. Remember to take account of sharps or flats accordingly.

2. Never use the same letter name together more than twice. For example G♭ - G♮ - G♯ would always be wrong. The G♯ note must be written as an A♭, or the G♭ should appear as an F♯. Much depends on the context in which you are working but remember, whatever happens, we never use the same letter name three in a row.

The key to easy transposition

Transposition simply means changing a given melody into another key or rewriting it either an octave higher or lower, usually on a different clef. At Grade 5 you only have to think about four different types of interval in transposition. You can be asked to transpose a melody upwards or downwards by:

- one octave
- a major 2nd
- a minor 3rd
- or a perfect 5th

We'll look at each in turn and see how it's done.

Transposing up or down by one octave

This is the easiest interval to deal with, because nothing changes *except the pitch*. It's an ideal opportunity for the examiner to test your knowledge of clefs, so let's begin by taking a fresh look at that clef positioning diagram, to help you remember how the clefs relate to one another.

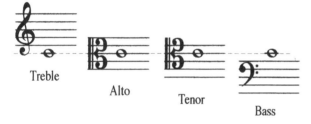

Treble   Alto   Tenor   Bass

Here's a scrap of tune. Let's say you are asked to transpose it down an octave and write it in the tenor clef.

If you follow this procedure, you can't really go wrong:

1. Look at that first note of G.

2. Consult the clefs diagram and locate where the note would appear *at the same pitch* on the tenor clef (on the first leger line above the stave, I think you'll agree).

3. Now locate where the G would appear one octave lower on the tenor clef (you should end up in the space between the second and third lines from the bottom).

4. Write your G crotchet in the correct position on the tenor stave accordingly. Once you're confident that your first note is at the correct pitch on the new clef, it's easy to follow the shape of the melody note for note. It becomes an exercise in accuracy, rather than knowledge.

You should end up with an answer that looks like this:

I play a C, you play a D. How come they sound the same?

If you're not a wind player, you may have glanced at the musical part of a neighbouring woodwind or brass player at orchestra rehearsal and wondered why he or she appears to be playing in a completely different key from everyone else.

That is because instruments such as clarinets, trumpets, french horns and cor anglais are what are called 'transposing' instruments, as opposed to instruments which play at *concert pitch*.

For example, if you play the note of middle C on the piano (concert pitch), the B flat clarinettist must play the note that he or she knows as D, in order to make the same note as the piano — because the clarinet's part is *transposed* upwards by a major 2nd.

Similarly, the french horn has to play G above middle C in order sound the same note, because its part is written a perfect 5th higher than concert pitch.

The reasons for these complications are technical and I'm glad to say we don't have to go into them here. But at Grade 5 we *are* expected to be able to score parts for transposing instruments.

The good news is that only three intervals need concern us — major 2nd for B flat instruments; minor 3rd for those in A; and perfect 5th for instruments in F.

Just as likely, you will be asked to transpose a melody *upwards* by an octave. If you met something like this…

… and you were told to transpose it up an octave into, say, the alto clef, you would simply follow the four-point procedure, but working upwards rather than downwards. The important thing is to fix the first note in the correct position; the rest follows easily from that.

Why not try the exercise in your manuscript book?

Things to watch out for:

• Students often make the mistake of rewriting the melody at the *same* pitch, which is why it's important to go through the measured steps which I've set out here.

• Another common mistake is to transpose the melody by two octaves. Again, working to the set procedure will help to avoid this problem.

• Make sure your new key signature is properly positioned on the stave. Pay particular attention to the tenor clef, which you will recall has its own special rule when setting out the sharps.

• Remember the upstems and downstems rule when transposing into another clef. The direction of stems is very likely to change, depending on the new clef.

Transposing into a different key

Just as we have a procedure for tackling octave transposition, we have another for transposing between keys — by a major 2nd, minor 3rd or perfect 5th.

An exam question may ask you to transpose upwards or downwards. You could be given a passage of music written for a particular transposing instrument and asked to re-score it as it would sound at concert pitch. Or vice versa. As with octave transposition, the key to success lies in getting the first note in its correct position — and then just accurately transposing the melody note for note.

Transposing a major second

Take a look at the following brief phrase. You are told that it is written at concert pitch and instructed to transpose it up a major 2nd (to be played by a B flat instrument).

Here's how to tackle it:

1. Identify the major key of the given passage. One flat tells us the key is F major.

2. Consult your keyboard diagram in order to find the new key. Count upwards (because we're transposing upwards) to establish the interval of a 2nd, *ie* from F to G. So we can tell that the new key is going to be a G *of some description*. We also know that a major second contains two semitones. The major second above F must be G *natural* — so the new key is G major.

3. Write out the major scale of the original key (F major) on a piece of scrap paper, and above it write the corresponding scale for the new key (G major). It helps avoid confusion if you place the scale of the *original* key *below* the scale of the new key if you are transposing upwards. And the other way about if transposing downwards:

Each pair of notes in the corresponding scales will be a major second apart. So the matrix of two scales together tells you everything you need to know (except for dealing with accidentals, but we'll come to that over the page).

4. Simply read off the notes from the matrix one by one. Wherever you see an A in the original, you know that the transposed melody must show a B; D becomes E, B♭ becomes C, and so on. So the solution must be:

And if you're transposing downwards, you can use the system in exactly the same way.

(continued overleaf)

Accident-free accidentals

The business of accidentals is easily dealt with. If, as in the example above, you encounter an accidental (and I can promise you the examiner will slip in a few to test you in any transposition question), you can easily make the necessary adjustment in your transposed version.

If the example is to be transposed up a major 2nd into G major, follow the process set out on the previous page:

G	A	B	C	D	E	F#	G
F	G	A	B♭	C	D	E	F

From the scales matrix we can see that the sharpened G must become a sharpened A, to preserve the major 2nd. The great thing about the matrix is that it helps you avoid the danger, in this instance, of writing a B♭ — which would sound the same of course, because it's an enharmonic equivalent of A#, but would be wrong because the interval between G# and B♭ is *not a major 2nd*.

The answer can only be:

Transposing a minor third

Now we can test the system again, this time by transposing *downwards* by a *minor 3rd*. Let's say the following few notes are from an orchestral part written for the A clarinet. We are told to rewrite the passage as it would actually sound at concert pitch (*ie* a minor 3rd lower).

Go through the set procedure:

1. What's the major key? Four flats; must be A♭ major.

2. What note is a minor 3rd lower than A♭? It has to be an F of some description (F-G-A is three letter names) and

we know that a minor 3rd always contains three semitones. So the key at concert pitch must be F major.

3. Write out the scale of A♭ major, with the scale of F major set out note-for-note *below* it (because we're transposing *downwards*).

A♭	B♭	C	D♭	E♭	F	G	A♭
F	G	A	B♭	C	D	E	F

4. Read off the notes from the matrix. As for the accidentals, the B♮ in the original (raised by a semitone) must become G# in the transposition (raised by a semitone). Similarly the restored B♭ (lowered by a semitone) must be G♮. So the answer looks like this:

Transposing a perfect fifth

Again it is a simple matter to transpose up or down a perfect 5th, using the same procedure. Here's a passage written at concert pitch; let's say the question asks us to transpose the melody up a perfect 5th so it would sound at concert pitch when played by the cor anglais.

1. The major key? D major.

2. Perfect 5th above D? The new key must be A major.

3. The matrix:

A	B	C#	D	E	F#	G#	A
D	E	F#	G	A	B	C#	D

4. So the correct answer is:

The long and the short of it

The scoring of vocal music written for four parts (soprano, alto, tenor and bass — or S, A, T, B) has special conventions and we have to know about this at Grade 5. There are two ways of writing for voices: in *short score* or in *open score*. You may be asked in the exam to rewrite a passage of vocal music from short score into open score or vice versa. So what do we mean by *short* and *open*?

In short score...

The vocal parts are written on two staves, treble and bass. The soprano and the alto share the treble stave; tenor and bass parts are written on the bass stave. In short score, vocal music would typically look like this:

There are a couple of things to note.

• See how the usual convention of upstems and downstems goes out the window here. Regardless of where the notes fall on the stave, the treble and tenor parts are written with upstems; the alto and bass with downstems. This is to help distinguish one voice's part from another and to prevent clashes between stems.

• The rules about accidentals (remember them from page 22?) apply to each part individually. In the example above, if the alto part included an F♯, as the soprano does, it would have to be marked as such. Strictly speaking an accidental in one part does not apply to any other part, but composers often mark in accidentals which are not technically necessary wherever there could be uncertainty.

In open score...

Each vocal part is written on a stave of its own. The soprano and alto parts use the treble clef and the bass is written in the bass clef. The rogue is the tenor part (always so troublesome, these tenors!) which is written in the treble clef — but *an octave higher* than its true pitch.

In the example above, see how the treble clef symbol in the tenor part has an *8* attached to its tail. This tells the tenors to sing an octave lower than written.

The example shows the same extract as that on the left, but in open score. Things to note are:

• The normal up/downstems rule *does* apply in open score, unlike the short score convention already discussed.

• The tenor part has its little *8* to show the part is written an octave higher than it sounds. Be specially careful with the tenor part; it's easy to make silly slips when transposing the part between open and short score.

Attention to detail

Have a look at the detail here also. If you are working on a blank stave, don't forget to add the bracket on the left-hand side which draws the parts together and the thinner line beside it which binds the staves together, whether there are two or four. Put in the S, A, T and B markings. And don't forget the little *8* on the tenors' treble clef.

When tackling a 'voices in score' question, you should include any dynamics, performance directions, slurs, ties and phrasing marks that appear in the original.

One other thing: be sure to keep the notes and bar lines for each part lined up vertically when you're writing your answer. It is most important that the eye can follow each beat of the bar vertically through the parts.

Keep it simple, make it musical

The requirement at Grade 5 is to compose a short melody, of not more than eight bars, for either an instrument or a voice. In the instrumental option you will be asked to write a melody for a particular instrument, or you may be given two or more instruments from which to choose. The voice alternative will provide you with a couple of lines from a poem which you have to set to music. In both cases, you will be expected to add performance directions.

Voice is the choice
Unless you are very good at hearing written music in your head, I recommend that you go for the voice option.

The instrumental question usually gives you an opening phrase of music by some well-known composer, which you then have to develop into something which follows that set style. (Personally I find it daunting to be asked to finish off a tune started by the likes of Bach or Mozart!)

The song alternative, on the other hand, is more flexible. Firstly, notes set to words tend to be less complicated because lines of verse often, but not always, have a helpful tumpty-tumpty rhythm to guide you.

Secondly, the voice option provides a definite framework, with a beginning, middle and end, so you know where you are. The other advantage is that no opening phrase of music is given, so you can start your tune however you think best. And you don't need to be an expert in the ranges of particular instruments or their peculiarities of bowing or articulation.

For all these reasons I am going to concentrate on showing you how to set words to music. However, if you are confident enough to tackle the instrumental option, I think you will still find most of what follows useful.

Hearing a melody in your mind's ear
Of course there will be no instruments to help you in the exam room. What you write all has to come out of your head. So how do you 'hear' when you have to keep silent?

We all know what a major scale sounds like. Try this: 'hum' a note under your breath (with a little practice you'll find it's quite easy to pitch an almost silent note in your mind). Perfect pitch doesn't come into this; just hum any middling sort of note and assume it's middle C.

Take your hummed note to be the tonic (C), and then silently hum a full octave of the major scale and back again to the tonic. You will find this simple technique invaluable when you're writing your tune on the stave.

Fixing intervals in your head
For the really important notes of the scale there are other little tricks which will help you 'hear'. The 5th (dominant), for example, can be located by silently humming the opening of *Twinkle Twinkle Little Star*. **Twink**-le **twink**-le. The first twink is the tonic; the second twink is the 5th. Try it now — but under your breath.

For the 3rd (mediant) and 4th (subdominant), hum the opening of *While Shepherds Watched Their Flocks By Night*. 'While' is the tonic; 'shep-herds' is the 3rd. And from 'their' (tonic) to 'flocks' provides a fix for the 4th.

When you have drafted out your tune in the exam, try the silent humming technique to check that it sounds as you intended before you firm it up as your finished piece. You may not have penned a musical classic, but at least you'll know that it does actually go how you meant it to.

These tricks will also make it easy to pitch the other notes of the scale in your mind's ear. Practice by thinking up some simple tunes and imagining them on the stave.

Getting the technical bit right
In composition there's never a specific 'right' answer. Some marks will certainly be awarded for inventiveness and imagination, but the most crucial issue is whether or not your offering hangs together technically.

This book can't help you write brilliant tunes, but it does aim to assist you in getting the technical bit right.

The two lines at the top of the next page (from a lyric I wrote called *The Angelus Bell*) provide us with a working model to show how to set about putting words to music. My advice, when you're writing melodies for exam purposes, is: keep it simple, make it musical.

Here's the drill.

1. Read the words through. Where do the natural accents fall? A **time** to sow, a **time** to reap, a **time** to turn the **plough**, and so on. You could also put lesser accents on *sow*, *reap* and *turn*. Now you can see where to put your bar lines, with the accents falling on the first beat of each bar. Write out the words on a piece of scrap paper and

A time to sow, a time to reap, a time to turn the plough;
A time for feast and dancing when the fruit hangs on the bough.

mark where the bar lines fall:

A |time to sow, a|time to reap, a|time to turn the|plough; A |time for feast and|**dan**-cing when the|**fruit** hangs on the|**bough**.

2. Time signature? Tap out the rhythm. The simplest solution is clearly four/four (four crotchet beats to the bar).

The first word, 'A', must be an upbeat of one crotchet, so the last bar on *bough* will have to contain only three crotchets, to compensate (just as *plough* at the end of the first line has to give the last beat of the bar to the '*A*' which begins the second line of verse).

3. Draw notes of the correct value above each syllable to suit your time signature.

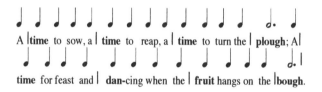

So far so good, but it's rather dull with those repetitive crotchets — and when I say 'keep it simple' I certainly don't mean 'make it dull'. So what can we do to spice things up? We could dot the crotchets where the accent falls on the first beat of the bar and slip in a pair of slurred quavers on the 'the' upbeats before the dotted minims:

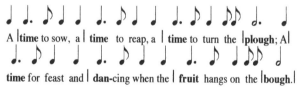

4. Read it through in rhythm. It has a nicely even shape, with the second line echoing the first. However, the dotted crotchet/quaver arrangement doesn't fit too well with the words on '*dan-cing*' or '*fruit hangs*', so let's put those two back as straight crotchets.

5. Now it's time to make a tune. My advice is to work in good old C major for simplicity. Keep your tune within one octave and avoid leaps of more than a 5th. Forget minor keys in order to avoid accidentals. In fact, don't use accidentals at all — unless you're super-confident.

Just as the rhythm must have shape and balance, so should the melody, with the second line sounding like a logical answering phrase to the first. The best way to achieve that is to land on the dominant at the half-way point (end of the first line — *plough*) and get back to the tonic for the last note, *bough*. Before you begin composing your tune, you can confidently write the dotted minim on *plough* as a G and plant a dotted minim C over *bough*.

6. Use the silent humming technique to compose your tune and write it on the stave — faintly in pencil until you're sure it sounds right.

7. It then remains to add your performance directions (look ahead to the relevant section on page 44).

You might end up with something like the solution shown below. Not the most dazzling composition ever, perhaps, but it's certainly workable and nobody could say it's 'wrong'. Well worth a few good marks!

Getting to grips with triads

Remember when we talked about intervals on page 24? What we didn't consider at that point was how those intervals actually *sound* when the two notes they contain are played at the same time. From your experience of playing music you will know how notes of different pitch combine to create musical harmony.

Now it's time to meet the 'triad' — a group of three notes played simultaneously to create a 'chord'. The triad provides the basic building block for all harmony.

Building triads

You can build a triad on any note of any scale, major or minor. The three notes the triad contains will always be:

The *root* (the note on which the triad is based)
The *3rd* above the root
The *5th* above the root

Let's see how these triads appear on the stave. Pick a key — let's say D major — but we'll do it without a key signature, with all the sharps shown, in order to make the construction of each triad quite clear:

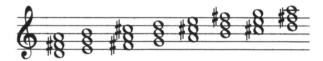

We know that every degree of the scale has a name:

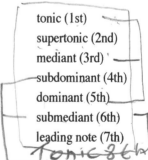

tonic (1st)
supertonic (2nd)
mediant (3rd)
subdominant (4th)
dominant (5th)
submediant (6th)
leading note (7th)

So it's natural that the triads built on them should take the same names. We talk of the 'tonic triad', the 'dominant triad', the 'supertonic triad' and so on, in any particular key. In *writing*, however, we usually refer to them by roman numerals, which represent the degrees of the scale:

I (tonic) **II** (supertonic) **III** (mediant) **IV** (subdominant)
V (dominant) **VI** (submediant) and **VII** (leading note).

One, two, four and five

The good news is that at Grade 5 we only have to consider four triads: the tonic (I), the supertonic (II), the subdominant (IV) and the dominant (V). Taking D major as our example again, the focus is on:

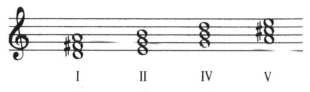

I   II   IV   V

Triads in minor keys

So far we've only talked about harmony in terms of major keys, but exactly the same principles apply to minor keys. And the same four chords (I, II, IV and V) apply.

One special thing to watch: the seventh degree (leading note) of the scale. You will remember that the seventh is sharpened in a harmonic minor scale. You may also have spotted that the leading note turns up in the dominant (V) triad. So where you have a dominant triad in a minor scale, *don't forget that accidental*. Here are our four triads in A minor (no sharps or flats in the key signature):

I   II   IV   V

Bear in mind what we learned about sharpened notes in minor scales on page 29. Once we get into minor keys of three or more *flats*, the accidental becomes a *natural*, rather than a sharp. And in minor keys with five or more *sharps* the accidental becomes a *double sharp*.

Let's first look at how this affects keys with three or more flats. If there is no key signature, there's no need to write a natural beside the leading note in the dominant triad. If there *is* a key signature, then the accidental is essential. Compare the examples below, showing the dominant triad of F minor. The first has a key signature so the leading note must be sharpened. But the second has no key signature, so an accidental is not necessary.

V

V

Now let's think about minor keys with five or more sharps. Consider the dominant (V) triad in the key of G♯ minor, first with, then without, a key signature:

In the first example the double-sharpened leading note is marked accordingly. In the second, even though there is no key signature, it still has to be marked double sharp. Note the congestion which can arise around triads with accidentals — another good reason for writing accidentals extremely accurately.

Inverted triads

The four triads we've discussed above are all said to be in *root position*. It is so-called because the note on which the triad is built (the *root*) is the lowest note of the three, with the 3rd and 5th stacked neatly on top.

'Inverted' triads are those in which the three notes are rearranged with either the 3rd or the 5th at the bottom.

 Look what happens when we put the 3rd of the triad (F♯) in the bass position. The 5th (A) can stay put, but the root (D) has to hop up an octave. With the 3rd at the bottom, the triad is said to be in its *first inversion.*

It follows that when the 5th takes the bottom place, we have the *second inversion.* In short:

Root position — root at the bottom
First inversion — 3rd at the bottom
Second inversion — 5th at the bottom

Notice how the intervals between the notes also change when the triad is inverted. Don't be confused by this. Though a triad might be in root position, first inversion or second inversion, its component notes remain the same — they have simply been rearranged and we continue to call them the root, 3rd and 5th wherever they may be placed.

The a-b-c of inversions

While we use roman numerals to identify the degree of the scale on which triads are built, we show whether they are in root position, first inversion or second inversion by adding an *a*, *b* or *c* to the roman numeral.

a = triad in root position
b = triad in first inversion
c = triad in second inversion

A tonic triad in first inversion is identified as I*b*, for example; the dominant in root position would be marked as V*a*; the subdominant in second inversion would be IV*c*, and so on.

Root position is often indicated by its roman numeral alone, dropping the *a*. However, I recommend that you always include the *a* if it's up to you, because it makes things that much more definite. But wherever you come across a roman numeral without a letter after it, you know you're looking at a triad in root position.

Triads by numbers

There is a second way of identifying the arrangement of triads. Instead of using the *a-b-c* method, some people prefer to use two numbers, one above the other after the roman numeral, to indicate the inversion of the triad. It's called 'figured bass' and it works like this:

$\frac{5}{3}$ = triad in root position
$\frac{6}{3}$ = triad in first inversion
$\frac{6}{4}$ = triad in second inversion

The numbers denote the intervals between the note on which the triad is built (root, 3rd or 5th) and the *upper two* notes in the triad. $\frac{5}{3}$ indicates that the upper notes are the 3rd and 5th (*ie* root position). $\frac{6}{3}$ tells us that the upper notes are arranged as a 3rd and a 6th above the note on which the triad is built (first inversion). And $\frac{6}{4}$ says that the upper notes are the 4th and 6th (second inversion).

So, for example, instead of writing II*b* to indicate a supertonic triad in first inversion you could convey the same message by expressing it as II$\frac{6}{3}$. As with the *a-b-c* system, a roman numeral alone indicates root position.

Confusingly, we still call the three notes of the triad the 'root', the '3rd' and the '5th' regardless of their relative positions in an inversion. This is particularly confusing in figured bass, where 6ths and 4ths enter the picture. But I'm afraid figured bass does sometimes crop up in Grade 5, so it's just something we have to learn and to live with.

Understanding chords in action

So far we have looked at groups of only three notes played simultaneously: triads. More loosely, we call these groups 'chords', but in practice chords tend to comprise more than three notes. One (sometimes more) of a triad's notes will be repeated elsewhere in the chord.

In the exam you could be asked to identify I (tonic), II (supertonic), IV (subdominant) and V (dominant) chords in any of the keys demanded at Grade 5 — that's major or minor keys up to six sharps or six flats. Chords may crop up in the exam in one of two ways:

Firstly, you will almost certainly be asked to identify particular chords in a passage of music written for three or four parts on two staves. Secondly, you will be required to suggest appropriate chords at given points in a melody.

How to identify chords

When we talked about short and open score on page 35, I commented on how important it is to write your notes in neat vertical alignment. Apart from making it easier for conductors, singers and players to read their parts, vertical alignment is essential because, of course, those four separate parts must work together to create *chords*.

Have another look at the following brief choral passage we studied in relation to voices in score. Consider the last three chords:

There's a set drill you should follow when you're asked to identify chords. If you always apply the following, you will find that naming them is quite simple.

1. *What's the key?* With two flats the key must be either B♭ or its relative minor, G minor.

And what is the first thing we suspect when we see an accidental — particularly a sharp with a key signature in flats? Yes, that sharp is most likely to be the leading note of the minor scale. If F♯ is the leading note, we know that

G must be the tonic. No question about it. This little excerpt is in the key of G minor.

2. *Write out the scale* (in letters). If you can't do it off the top of your head, then set out the basic model of A minor (no sharps or flats in the key signature) and then transpose the same intervals on to a minor scale starting on the note of G. If you don't arrive at this...

G   A   B♭   C   D   E♭   F♯   G

... then there's something seriously adrift, but I have every confidence that you have it right!

3. *Number the notes in roman numerals.* As you know, we only have to consider I (tonic), II (supertonic), IV (subdominant) and V (dominant), so let's immediately discount the rest by marking only those which concern us:

G   A   B♭   C   D   E♭   F♯   G
I   II   IV   V   I

Remember that each chord will contain three notes: its root (on which the chord is built), and the 3rd and 5th above the root.

4. *Analyse the chords.* Look first at the notes which make up the final chord in the example. You will see we have G in the bass, B♭ in the tenor, D in the alto and G again in the soprano. A look at the model of G minor above shows that there is only one chord which contains the three notes of G, B♭ and D: it has to be the tonic.

Thus we know that the final chord of the piece is the tonic chord, but we also have to decide whether it is in root position or in an inversion. Clearly, with G (the tonic) in the bass, this must be in root position (**Ia**).

Now what about the chord which precedes it? The notes which make it are D (twice), A and F♯. Consult the model — what is the only chord to which these three notes belong? It must be V (dominant). And with D in the bass, it must be in root position (**Va**).

The third chord from the end also has D in the bass, but its other notes are B♭, G and another D. A glance at the model shows that only the tonic chord contains those three notes, but with the 5th (D) in the bass we must be talking second inversion, so in shorthand it's **Ic**.

If you analyse chords in this way, you should have no trouble with naming them accurately.

Putting chords to work at cadences

As well as being able to identify chords at Grade 5, we also have to be able to *use* chords. You may be asked in the exam to suggest chords to accompany a melody where 'cadences' — sort of musical punctuation — occur at the ends of musical phrases.

At the end of a tune, we want it to sound like the end, so we use chords that finish up on the tonic. The most emphatic sounding ending would be for the last two chords to be the dominant (V) followed by the tonic (I).

In the middle of the piece, we'd normally want the chords to tell the listener that there's more to follow, so we'd certainly avoid using the tonic. The most likely chord would be the dominant (V) with a I, II or IV just before it.

There are three types of cadence we need to know:

V followed by I is called a 'perfect' cadence.
IV followed by I is called a 'plagal' cadence.
I-V, II-V or IV-V is called an 'imperfect' cadence.

If you look back at the section on composing a melody (page 36/37) you will see how we accentuated the end of each line. These are the cadential points in the piece and they need the right treatment with chords in order to make the line endings sound right to the ear.

At Grade 5 the tunes to be harmonised will be written in either C, G, D or F major (no minors at this grade).

We also only have to concern ourselves with the four types of chord: the tonic (I), the supertonic (II), the sub-dominant (IV) and the dominant (V).

Here again are the last two bars of the first line of our composition — the mid-way point of the melody:

What would be a suitable cadence at this half-way mark? As the key signature suggests, the tune is certainly in C major. Jot down the notes of the scale:

C D E F G A B C

In which chords (I, II, IV or V) does the note of G appear? Only in the tonic chord (I) and the dominant (V).

Since we are at the half-way mark here, we wouldn't want to use the tonic chord, because that would make it sound as if the tune was ending. But a dominant chord would be ideal, indicating that there's more to come.

A cadence is always made up of at least two chords, so what about the chord to precede our V? In the previous bar we have the notes C, D, E, D, C. Ignore the short D notes for a moment; they are called 'passing notes' and we'll talk about them in a moment. The principal notes are C and E, both of which appear in the tonic chord, so the whole of that bar could be harmonised with a I chord, creating an imperfect cadence with the V.

Our cadence could go like this:

Now think about the end of the melody (ignore the C passing note for a moment). You should be able to see how it finishes on a perfect cadence, like this:

Passing notes and auxiliary notes

Short melody notes which don't feature in the chord, but which link two notes which do belong in the chord, are called 'passing' notes. They don't have to be considered when harmonising.

You will also encounter what are known as 'auxiliary' notes. Like passing notes, they don't actually figure in the chord. When a melody note is played twice, and the next note above or below it is sounded in between, that middle note is called an auxiliary note.

In the example shown below the A in the first triplet and the E in the second are both auxiliary notes.

Reading the signs

Ornament symbols, a form of musical shorthand, are relics of the olden days when the process of reproducing written music was very much more complicated than it is now. To save the scribe or the printer from writing out or engraving long strings of notes, composers would use a system of symbols to indicate to the player how a particular note or groups of notes should be played.

There are five types of ornament symbols that we have to be able to recognise and interpret at Grade 5:

- turns (and inverted turns)
- mordents (and inverted mordents)
- trills (also known as shakes)
- acciaccaturas (short grace notes)
- appoggiaturas (long grace notes)

The turn

With its symbol looking like an S on its side, a turn written directly over a note tells us to divide its value into four and play the note above it, the note itself, the note below it and the note itself again, like this:

If the turn is placed *after* a note, divide that note in half, then treat its second half in the same way as shown above, like this:

Ornaments with accidentals

A turn with an accidental above it, below it, or both above and below tells a fairly obvious story. For example:

means play the upper note of the turn as a sharp

means play the lower note of the turn as a natural

means play the upper note flat and lower sharp

The inverted turn

The symbol for the inverted turn is the same S shape on its side, but with a line through it. The inverted turn behaves in exactly the same way as the regular turn, except that the turn goes round the other way:

An inverted turn placed *after* a note performs just the same way as its counterpart regular turn — except that it is inverted, of course — and what we discussed about accidentals also applies here.

Mordents and inverted mordents

Sometimes these are known as upper and lower mordents. The symbol for the ordinary (upper) mordent is a neat squiggle written over the note to which it applies. It tells the player to throw in two demisemiquavers at the beginning of the note, like this:

It won't come as any surprise to learn that an inverted (lower) mordent follows the same pattern, but the other way up. Its symbol is the same squiggle, but it has a line through it, and it is played as follows:

The only other thing to say is that upper mordents can carry an accidental above, and lower mordents below, in the same style as for turns (see left). An accidental will affect the upper or lower note accordingly.

The trill or shake

Something of a specialist subject, the trill or shake. There are a number of variants that have to be taken into account when interpreting *tr* written above a note. Even the period in which the piece was composed can make a difference. In fact there is so much uncertainty that, for Grade 5 purposes, we cover only the basics.

Essentially, a trill is an alternation of the given note and the one above it. It begins on the note above the given note and ends with a turn, bringing in the note below the given note. Probably easier to understand when you see it:

Sometimes you will come across a trill symbol with a long wavy line after it (*tr*~~~~) particularly where a trill is applied to a minim or longer note. It means exactly the same as the plain trill symbol.

The acciaccatura (pronounced at-chiak-a-toora)

This is the short grace note, distinguished by the little diagonal line through its stem and tail. No doubt you have come across the acciaccatura in your playing. The small note is played as a demisemiquaver and its value subtracted from the value of the given note:

The appoggiatura (pronounced a-podja-toora)

A longer grace note, written as a small note like the acciaccatura but without the line through its stem and tail. The value of an appoggiatura is generally taken to be half the value of the note to which it's applied. Thus:

There are also double — sometimes triple — grace notes, but it's rare for these to appear at Grade 5.

Repetitions

Various signs are used to indicate a repetition of a note or notes. For example, rather than write out a row of quavers, a composer might use the following device:

Or if the repetition involves semiquavers, two stripes through the stem tell the story, like this:

Two minims beamed together might look a bit off the wall, but this has a meaning which you ought to know:

The composer could also direct chords to be repeated by using a 'slash' symbol to show the number of repetitions:

The following symbols say (fig 1) play the preceding bar again or (fig 2) play the preceding bar twice:

And sections of music to be repeated are contained within double bar lines with dots, as shown here:

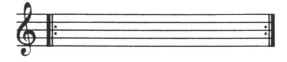

Following the directions

More symbols and signs

𝆮. ❀ or 𝒫_____ is an instruction to pianists to step on the right-hand pedal. The star, or the end of the bracket, is placed where the pedal is to be released.

Known by musicians as a 'hairpin' the following symbol means crescendo (get louder) and spans the notes to which it applies: ◁==========

Decrescendo or diminuendo (get quieter) uses the same hairpin symbol, but in reverse: ==========▷

String players have special signs to tell them in which direction they should use the bow. ⊓ drawn above a note means you should begin on a down bow and a V above the note indicates that you should begin on an up bow.

In music for wind instruments the V symbol is used to indicate where the player should take a breath.

'Staccato' means playing a note very short; it is indicated by a dot placed above or below (depending on whether the stem is upwards or downwards) the note. It looks like this: ♩̣ or this: ˙♩

When notes have staccato dots, but are joined by a slur, it means play the notes staccato but don't overdo it.

A note with a little triangle over it means you should make the staccato especially pronounced: ▾♩

The instruction to accentuate a note comes in two strengths. >♩ indicates that the note should be accented, while ˅♩ says you should really lay into it.

A straight dash above a note indicates that it should be played with a slight emphasis: ─♩

The symbol of a semicircle with a dot in the middle indicates a pause on the note marked: ⌢♩

All these symbols can be used either above or below the note, depending on the direction of the stem.

Some common abbreviations

As we have seen, music is full of shorthand symbols. Here we round up the most common word abbreviations.

f	*forte*	loud
ff	*fortissimo*	very loud
fff	*fortissimo*	very loud indeed
fp	*forte piano*	loud then immediately quiet
mf	*mezzo forte*	moderately loud
p	*piano*	quiet
pp	*pianissimo*	very quiet
ppp	*pianissimo*	very quiet indeed
mp	*mezzo piano*	moderately quiet
rf or *rfz*	*rinforzando*	heavily stressed/accented
fz	*forzando*	with force
sf or *sfz*	*sforzando*	loudly accented
D.C.	*da capo*	go back to the beginning
D.S.	*dal segno*	go back to the sign 𝄋
pizz.	*pizzicato*	pluck (for string players)
rall.	*rallentando*	becoming gradually slower
rit.	*ritardando*	becoming gradually slower
cresc.	*crescendo*	becoming gradually louder
decresc.	*decrescendo*	becoming gradually quieter
dim.	*diminuendo*	becoming gradually quieter
ten.	*tenuto*	hold the note

Setting the tempo

Most musical compositions begin with an indication of the tempo at which the composer directs the piece should be played. Here's a collection of the most common directions, with an interpretation of what each means and an approximate metronome guide.

prestissimo	extremely fast	♩ = 200-208
presto	fast	♩ = 168-200
allegro	fast and lively	♩ = 125-168
allegretto	quite fast	♩ = 116-125
moderato	moderate speed	♩ = 108-116
andantino	brisk walking speed	♩ = 90-108
andante	walking speed	♩ = 76-90
adagio	slowly	♩ = 70-76
lento	very slowly	♩ = 66-70
larghetto	less slowly than largo	♩ = 60-66
largo	slow and stately	♩ = 40-60

Changing the pace of the piece

As you will know from your playing, composers often want to vary the pace of the music. Here are some of the more common words they use to let the player know.

accelerando	getting faster
ritardando (rit.)	getting gradually slower
rallentando (rall.)	getting gradually slower
allargando	make it broader
ritenuto (rit., riten.)	slow up, hold back
più mosso	more movement
meno mosso	less movement
a tempo	return to the previous speed
tempo primo	return to the original speed

Some of the more common performance directions

a capella	unaccompanied (voices)
agitato	agitated
alla	in the manner of
amoroso	lovingly
anima, con anima	soulfully
animato	animated
appassionato	passionately
arco	use the bow (string players)
assai	very
attacca	go straight on
bravura	boldness
brillante	brilliant
brioso, con brio	with vigour
cantabile	in a singing style
coda	an ending to the music
col, coll, con	with
da	from
da capo	from the beginning
dolce	sweetly
dolente	sadly
dolore	sorrow
espressivo	with expression
fine	end
forza	force
fuoco	fire
furioso	furiously
giocoso	playfully

giusto	proper, exact
glissando	sliding
grandioso	grandly
grave	solemn
grazioso	gracefully
lacrimoso	sadly, tearfully
legato	smoothly
leggiero	lightly
lugubre	doleful, mournful
lunga pausa	long pause
ma	but
maestoso	majestically
marcia	in marching style
meno	less
mezzo	half
molto	much, a lot
mosso	movement
non	not
non troppo	not too much
ossia	or
pastorale	country style
pausa	pause
più	more
poco	a little
poco a poco	little by little
prima volta	first time
primo	first
rubato	in free time
scherzando	playfully
scherzo	a joke
senza	without
simile	similarly
sordini	mutes
sostenuto	sustained
spiccato	jerky, detached
spiritoso	spiritedly
subito	suddenly
tacet	silence
tempo	time
tempo giusto	strict time
tranquillo	peacefully
tutti	all together
vivace	lively, vivacious
volti subito (V.S.)	turn the page quickly

The target is 66 – or 90 for a distinction

So now you're an expert — it's time to sit the exam! I suggest that, in the run-up to taking your Grade 5, you get a copy of the most recent past papers from your music shop and work through them. The Associated Board publishes these annually and each edition contains four papers.

What to take into the exam

Naturally, you won't be allowed to take in books or any other reference materials. You should have with you:

- HB pencils (always carry at least one spare)
- pencil sharpener
- short ruler
- eraser (get a good quality one)

You won't be allowed to take scrap paper into the exam. The invigilator will provide you with plenty of blank manuscript paper for all your workings out.

How to tackle the exam

You get two hours to complete your answers, which is plenty of time for anyone who's worth a pass. The paper is marked out of 100. For a pass you must score a minimum 66; and 90 marks or better secures a distinction.

• *Read the questions carefully.* The Grade 5 exam comprises seven questions. Read each question extremely carefully before you set about answering it, to ensure that you understand exactly what is being asked. Wouldn't it be a tragedy to score no marks on a particular section simply because you failed to read the question properly?

• Before you start work, draw out your keyboard diagram on the manuscript paper; also the clefs diagram which we studied on page 6, plus the intervals matrix (page 25) and the scale models for C major and A minor. The Circle of Fifths is also certain to be a useful reference.

• Don't do your workings out on the exam paper itself. They should be done on the manuscript paper provided. Only your answers should appear on what you hand in.

• Write as clearly as you possibly can. A neatly presented exam paper will help get the examiner on your side — and that could easily make a difference if your marks are borderline, whether for a pass or a distinction.

• When writing an answer to a question, do it faintly at first. Only when you have checked your answer is absolutely correct — and then checked it again — should you mark in your answer more boldly. Rubbing out heavy pencil marks always leaves a messy splodge, no matter how hard you scrub away with an eraser.

• Answers written in pencil are perfectly acceptable. So I'd advise you not to ink in your answers with a pen, just in case you spot something wrong at the last minute.

• Take the full two hours allowed. Take it easy, take your time, pace yourself. If you stay calm you're much less likely to get hassled into getting something wrong.

And finally...

I hope *Take Five* has helped you with your Grade 5 Theory studies. I have enjoyed writing it and I hope my enthusiasm for theory has been infectious. Most of all I hope that your studies and hard work bring you success. A pass is all you need — but I wish you a distinction!

May all your music bring you joy

Chris Dunn